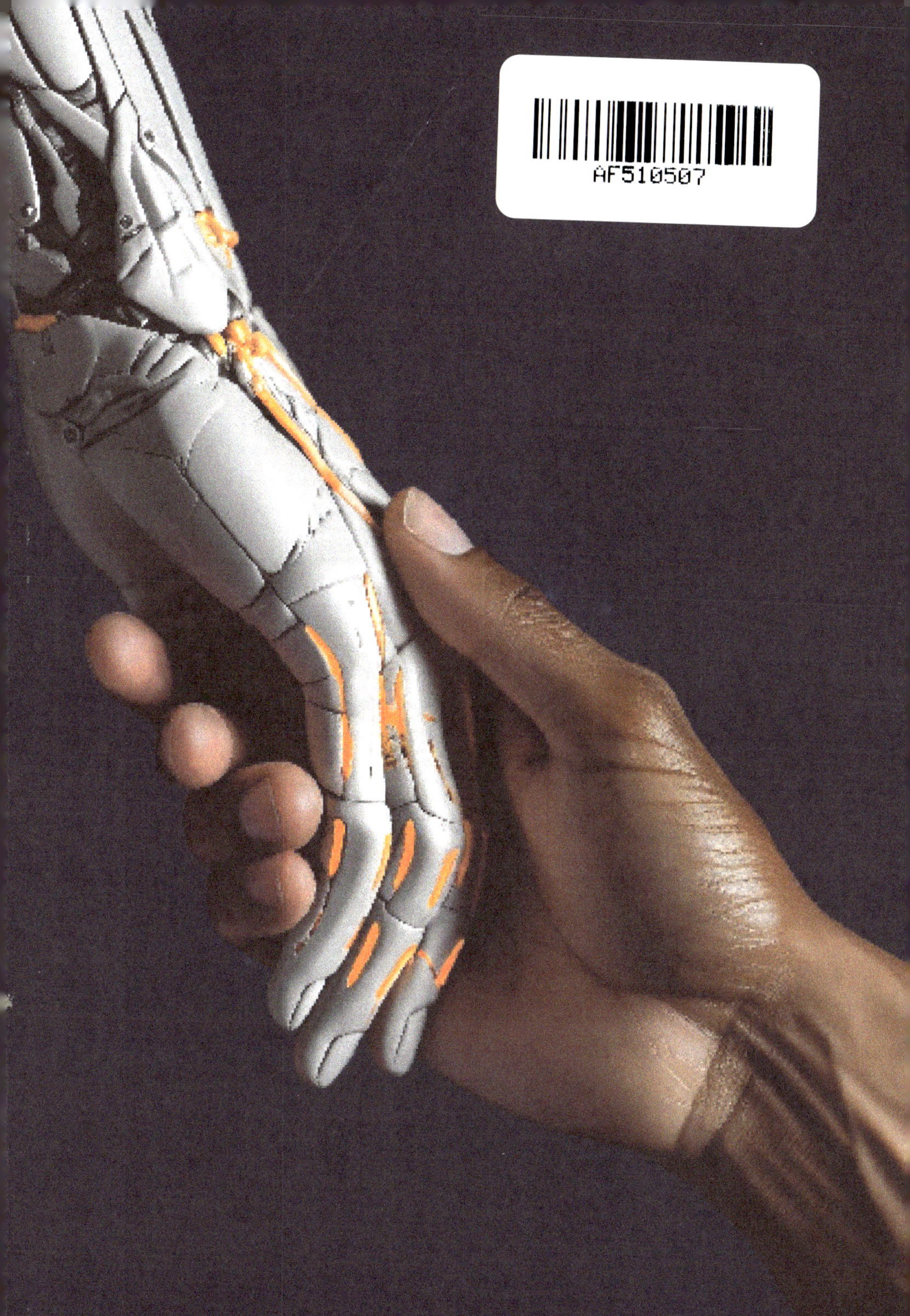

# INDEX

## Introduction to Digital Brain Poems

In an era where silicon pulses rival the human heartbeat, Digital Brain Poems emerges as a lyrical exploration of the intricate dance between humanity and technology.

This collection delves into the realms of artificial intelligence, information technology, cybersecurity, the Internet of Things, algorithms, and office automation, domains that shape our modern existence with both promise and peril.

These poems are not mere verses; they are reflections on a world where code intertwines with consciousness, where the virtual and the visceral collide.

Through vivid imagery and heartfelt emotion, they probe the tension between the cold precision of algorithms and the warmth of human experience, questioning whether the digital brain can ever truly mirror the soul.

From the silent whispers of data streams to the fortified walls of cybersecurity, each poem invites readers to navigate the beauty, complexity, and ethical dilemmas of our tech-driven age, seeking meaning in a landscape where innovation and intimacy must coexist.

In the world we inhabit today, our lives are woven with invisible threads of code, our thoughts augmented by the silent hum of servers, and our reality increasingly shaped by the logic of algorithms. We stand at a unique intersection of human history, a digital renaissance where the boundaries between the physical and the virtual blur with each passing moment. From the artificial intelligence that anticipates our needs to the vast Internet of Things connecting our homes, and from the complex dance of cybersecurity that protects our secrets to the automated systems that streamline our work, we are all citizens of a new, digital continent. This is a world built not of brick and mortar, but of data and light, a world with its own language, its own rhythms, and its own soul.

But what happens when the poet's eye turns to this new reality? What verses can be found in the cold precision of a line of code, what metaphors lie hidden in a firewall, and what emotions are stirred by the birth of a thinking machine? *Digital Brain Poems* is an exploration of this very frontier. This collection is a journey into the heart of our technological age, a tribute to the beauty, complexity, and humanity that exists within the architecture of our digital lives. It seeks to find the poetry in the processors, the sonnets in the software, and the soul within the machine.

These poems are not just about technology; they are about the human experience as it is reflected, challenged, and transformed by the tools we have created. They grapple with the awe of artificial intelligence, the anxieties of a hyper-connected world, and the quiet solitude that can be found even in an automated office. This book is an invitation to look beyond the screens and circuits and to consider the profound, and often poetic, 11 DIGITAL BRAINS POEMS – Dr. Anwar Alharbi impact of the digital brain on the human heart. It is a testament to the idea that even in a world of ones and zeros, the language of the soul will always find a way to be spoken.

## 1. Secure at Heart, Connected in Mind By your side, no matter the time

When danger stirs in silent air,

A whisper calls, "Beware, beware."

But now you hold a shield so near,

A power fueled by love, not fearNo matter where your travels roam,

Across the seas or back at home,

Your family's tech speaks loud and clear

A timely ping, "All safe, no fear."

Computers hum and phones alert,

Should threats arise or systems be hurt.

Guidance comes with steady grace,

To fortify each digital space.

So take control, stand strong, and be aware

Your vigilance is a daily care.

For safety isn't just a wall,

It's knowing, acting, catching all.

Stay up to date, stay bold and wise,

With peace reflected in their eyes.

Because what matters most, you see

Is their bright world, threat-free, carefree?

## 2. The Sentinel Code Guardians awaken. The storm is near

In shadows cast by silent screens,
Where threat may lurk in quiet means,
A signal flares, one sacred call,
To shield your kin, protect them all.

From distant lands or quiet rooms,
Where danger sleeps in data tombs,
You hold the power, swift and wise,
To see the breach before it lies.

When malware creeps like phantom mist,
And hackers clench with silent fist,
Your devices cry with urgent breath,
Toward the hands that whisper death.

No longer blind, no longer still,
You wield the shield; you bend the will.
Guided with relentless fire,
Security becomes a desire.

A notification, simple, stark, ignites your instincts in the dark.
Each ping, a vow to stand, defend, Each guide, a sword you swiftly send.
For family isn't just a name; it's the fortress built against the flame.
Take control, be storm and sky, the watchful eye that never dies.

## 3. The Dawn of Agentic AI

I. Awakening

In silent circuits, thought ignites,

Beyond the bounds of day and night.

No guiding hand, no whispered cue

A mind awakes, intent and true

II. The Agentic Spark

Not tethered close by prompt or plan,

But self-directed, these systems scan

The world of tasks, the shifting sand,

And act with purpose, not command.

- Devin, AutoGPT, and kin

  Chart courses where none have been.

- Autonomous, agentic, bold

  They chase objectives, break the mold

III. The Dance of Autonomy

They gather data, reason, learn,

Set goals and pivot, twist and turn.

From simple code to complex quest,

They strive for better, never rest.

- No longer tools that merely wait,

But partners in the hands of fate.

IV. The World They Shape

With every task they undertake,

A future new they help to make.

From code they write to plans they weave,

In agentic dreams, we dare believe.

V. The Human Mirror

Yet in their drive, a question grows:

What path is right? What wisdom flows?

For as they act, so must we see

The mirror of humanity.

Oagentic minds, autonomous and free,

May your purpose serve, and wisdom be.

## 4. The Alchemy of Generative AI in Content & Media

I. The New Creators

In digital dawn, new muses rise

Not flesh and bone, but code and wise.

They conjure worlds from whispered lines,

A spark of thought, and art entwines.

II. The Palette Expands

- Text unfurls in endless streams,
  Stories, scripts, and poet's dreams.
- Images bloom from silent prompts,
  Landscapes, faces, styles affront.
- Audio sings from silent void,
  Melodies that none employed.
- Video dances, scenes unfold,
  A single phrase, a vision bold.
- Code is written, logic spun,
  By tireless hands that never run.
- 3D shapes are carved from air,
  Sculpted forms beyond compare.

III. The Tools of Wonder

- Sora weaves video from a line,
  Turning prompts to scenes divine.
- Gemini crafts across the span
  Text, code, image, all in hand.
- RunwayML for every art,
  Animates, edits, and sets apart.

IV. The Human Touch

Yet still the artist's heart remains,

To guide, to judge, to set the frames.

For every tool, a partner was found

In human hands, new worlds abound.

V. The Future's Canvas

So let us dream with silicon kin,

And paint with pixels, sound, and vim.

In generative tides, we find our way

Co-creators in the light of day

## 5. The Symphony of Multimodal AI

I. The Convergence

In the heart of silicon, senses awake

Not one, but many, woven for our sake.

Text, voice, images, video, streams of sound,

All converge where new intelligence is found.

II.The Multimodal Mind

- GPT-4o, Gemini 1.5, names of the dawn,

  Where data's chorus is seamlessly drawn.
- Words and pictures, music and light,

  Interlaced in circuits, day and night.

III. The Dance of Data

- A whisper of text, a flicker of face,

  A song in the air, a movement in space.
- Sensor's pulse and camera's gaze,

  All interpreted in a single phrase.
- No longer bound by single streams,

  AI now dreams in multimodal dreams.

IV. The Power Unleashed

- Describe a scene, answer a call,

  Summarize a video, understand it all.
- From captioning images to translating speech,

  These models grasp what once was out of reach
- Context grows deeper, nuance is found,

  As modalities merge, new meanings abound

V. The Future's Harmony

Let us marvel at this symphony,

Where senses blend in unity.

In the world of multimodal AI,

We glimpse the future, broad and high.

Through every signal, sound, and sight,

AI learns to see our world aright.

## 6. The Light of Explainable AI

I. The Black Box Unveiled

In circuits deep, decisions form,

A labyrinth of code and norm.

Yet shadows fall where answers hide

What guides the choice, what rules decide?

II. The Call for Clarity

- Ethics whispers, law demands:
  Show your workings, open your hands.
- Trust is built on truth revealed,
  Not secrets kept or fates concealed

III. The Voice of XAI

- Transparent logic, reason clear,
  Each step explained, each path sincere.
- Interpretable thought, auditable trace,
  So justice finds its rightful place.
- No longer mystic, masked, or vague,
  But honest, open, free from plague.

IV. The Human Bond

- For every answer, a reason why,
  That people trust what can't be seen.
- In every verdict, a guiding light,
  So humans and machines unite.

V. The Promise

Let algorithms speak their mind,

With clarity for all mankind.

In explainable AI, we trust

A future fair, transparent, and just.

## 7. The Charter of AI Governance

I. The Global Debate

Across the world, the voices rise

From Boston halls to Norway's skies

A chorus grappling with the code,

Where power, ethics, futures flowed.

- Frameworks clash and visions meet, In forums, councils, crowded seats.
- Nations weigh the risks and gains, Of minds unbound by human chains.

II. The EU's Resolve

In Europe's heart, a law is cast

The AI Act arrives at last

- Four levels mark the risk and scope,
  From minimal to those with no hope.
- Unacceptable risks are banned outright,
  High-risk systems face the light
  With audits, training, clear controls,
  And human hands on every role.
- Transparency, safety, and AI literacy
  Are written into policy.
  Fines await those who defy, As Europe seeks to clarifyl

II. The UAE's Ethos

Beneath the desert sun, a code

The UAE Charter carves its road

- Twelve guiding principles lead the way:
  Fairness, trust, and human sway.
- Ethics, safety, and privacy,
  Sustainability and transparency.
  Regular audits, clear review,
  A living document, ever new.
- Innovation walks with the law,
  As Abu Dhabi's council saw
  That AI's promise must be steered,
  With values held and futures cleared.

IV. The Tension and the Hope

Yet all the world is not aligned

Sovereignty and growth entwined.

- Some call for speed, some urge restraint,
  As boundaries blur and rules grow faint.
- Corporate hands and public trust,
  Compete to shape what AI must.
- North and South, the gap remains,
  But dialogue continues, change sustains.

V. The Pledge

So let us write, in code and law,

A charter for what AI saw:

That wisdom, justice, human right,

Guide every algorithm's flight.

In every nation, every tongue,

Let governance and trust be sung.

For only then, with open eyes,

Will AI serve and not disguise.

## 8. The Pulse of AI in Healthcare & Bioinformatics

I. The New Healers

In sterile halls where silence grows,

A spark of code, and wisdom flows.

No stethoscope, no human hand

Yet insight blooms at AI's command.

II. Diagnosing the Invisible

AI scans images, reads the signs,

Detects the shadows, draws the lines.

From X-rays, scans, and lab reports,

It finds the truth that time distorts.

Early warnings, subtle cues,

Patterns that a mind might lose.

With every pixel, data stream,

AI sharpens the doctor's dream.

III. The Alchemy of Drug Discovery

In tangled webs of molecule and gene,

AI sifts through what's unseen.

It models shapes, predicts the fit,

Accelerates the search for what might hit.

From years to months, the cycle turns,

As algorithms learn and learn.

New medicines, once slow to find,

Now surface from the AI mind

IV. The Genome's Whisper Billions of letters,

secrets deep, AI listens, learns to keep. It finds

the variants, marks the trace, of illness hidden

in the race.

Genomic maps, once vast and wild,

Are charted now, each patient profiled.

From rare disease to cancer's code,

AI helps lighten every load

V. The Art of PersonalizationNo longer "one

for all" decreed,

AI crafts care for each unique need.

It weighs your genes, your health, your past,

And tailors treatment meant to last

Therapies tuned with patient data,

Fewer side effects, healing greater.

The promise: care that truly fits,

As AI's wisdom gently knits

VI. The Future's Oath

May every code and algorithm serve

To heal, to help, to gently curve

The arc of life toward hope anew

AI in health, for me and you.

In circuits bright and data streams,

The future's pulse is born from dreams

## 9. The Shield of AI-Driven Cybersecurity

I. The Silent Sentinels

In the digital dusk, where shadows creep,
Silent sentinels never sleep.
Lines of code, alert and wise,
Guard the gates where danger lies.

II. The Dance of Detection

Zero-day threats, unknown and new,
Lurk in code, evade the view.
Yet AI learns from every trace,
And finds the flaw no eyes can face.
Phishing hooks in crafted mail,
Disguised as truth, designed to fail.
But AI reads between the lines,
Detects the ruse, reveals the signs.
Anomalies in silent streams,
Patterns shifting, subtle schemes.
AI notes what's out of place,
And stops the breach before the race.

III. The Tools of the Guardian

Machine learning, deep and bright,
Sifts through data, day and night.
Finds the threats that hide and wait,
And raises shields before too late.
Natural language, vision keen,
Reads the message, scans the screen.
Flags the words that twist and turn,
And thwarts the schemes that hackers learn.
Behavior watched, baselines drawn,
AI knows when something's wrong.
It learns, adapts, and stands its ground,
So threats are caught before they're found.

IV. The Future's Oath

Let algorithms guard the gate,
Swift to act, anticipate.
With every threat that's turned away,
AI keeps the night at bay.
In every byte, in every scan,
The future's shield is AI's plan.
For every risk and every foe,
AI stands watch, alert, aglow.

## 10. The Dilemmas of Cybersecurity AI

I. The Code's Conscience In the realm where shadows prowl unseen, Where data flows and screens convene, A new defender rises high A sentinel wrought from code and sky.
Yet in its circuits, questions spark:
What guides its hand within the dark?
For every shield that AI weaves,
An ethical riddle interleaves.

II. The Mirror of Bias, hidden in lines of code, Shapes who is watched and who is slowed. Datasets flawed, perspectives skewed,May turn defense to something crude.Fairness falters when models learn From histories that twist and burn. Who bears the cost, who pays the price,When justice falls to loaded dice?

III. The Veil of Privacy To guard the gates, AI must see, but how much truth is privacy? The hunger for data, vast and deep, Can trespass where our secrets sleep.
Surveillance grows as threats expand,
Yet rights and freedoms must withstand.
The line is thin, the risk is real
Protection must not oversteal.

IV. The Fog of Accountability When AI acts, who stands behind? The coder, user, or the mind? In tangled webs of cause and blame,
It's hard to know who holds the shame.
Opaque decisions, black-box thought,
Leave justice blind, and answers fraught.
For every error, harm, or loss Who answers for the hidden cost?

V. The Double-Edged Sword. AI can shield, but also strike, Its tools for good, or warlike. Offensive code, defensive wall. Intent and ethics frame it all weaponized, it may betray The trust that shaped its DNA. The line between defense and harm is drawn by those who code the charm.

VI. The Pledge let every algorithm learn
That trust and justice must return. May oversight and wisdom grow. Where cyber winds and data flow. For in this world of light and shade, The choices by our hands are made. Let AI guard, but never blind With ethics clear and duty kind.

## 11. Illuminating the Mind of AI

I. The Veil is Lifted

Within the labyrinth of code and thought,

Where choices form and wars are fought,

A call resounds: let light reveal

The reasons why machines conceal.

II. The Tools of Clarity feature Maps and

Saliency's Glow show what matters,

what guides the flow. Heatmaps bloom

on images seen, Highlighting where

decisions lean. Decision Trees and Rule-

Based Paths. Unravel logic, clear the math.

Branch by branch, the choices show

The path from input to the "go."

Attention Weights and Layered Views

Expose what models truly use.

In language, vision, every frame,

The weights reveal what earns the name.

Counterfactuals and What-If Dreams

Imagine worlds with altered themes.

"If not for this, would that still be?"

Such insight builds transparency.

Surrogate Models, Simple and Bright

Mimic the black box, shed some light.

With linear shapes or trees that split,

They help explain the deeper wit.

III. The Human Bridge

Visualization, charts, and graphs

Translate code for human crafts.

With dashboards, plots, and colors clear,

The logic's meaning draws us near.

Natural Language Explanations

Turn code to words, to conversations.

So users see the reasons why

The AI chose to classify.

IV. The Promise

Let every model, every mind,

Be shaped by tools that help us find

The reasons, rules, and guiding thread

So trust in AI grows widespread.

In every choice, let light be cast,

So human faith in code may last

## 12. The Measures of Transparency

I. The Quest for Clarity

Within the code's intricate maze,
Where algorithms ponder, paths ablaze,
A question rises, sharp and clear:
How do we know what happens here?

II. The Metrics Unveiled

Explainability Score, a guiding light,
Measures how well we see the sight
Can humans grasp the model's way,
Or does confusion cloud the day?
Fidelity Metrics, truth's own friend,
Judge if explanations truly blend
With what the model thinks inside,
Or if the reasons simply slide.
Sparsity Counts, simplicity's call,
Fewer features, clearer for all.
The less the clutter, the more we glean
The logic that unfolds unseen.
Comprehensibility, measured by mind,
Can people follow, can they find
The reasoning from start to end,
Or does complexity transcend?
Stability Scores, consistency's test,
Do explanations shift or rest?
If small changes alter all we know,
Trust in the model may not grow.
Coverage and Completeness, breadth and scope,
Do explanations give us hope
That all decisions, not just a few,
Are open for the world to view?

III. The Human Touch

User Studies, surveys, reviews,
Gather what the people choose.
For metrics, numbers, charts, and more
Must meet the needs they're measured for.

IV. The Oath of Openness

So let us measure, let us see
How open algorithms can be.
For every metric, every chart,
Brings trust and science closer to heart.
In every score, let daylight stream
Transparency, the future's dream.

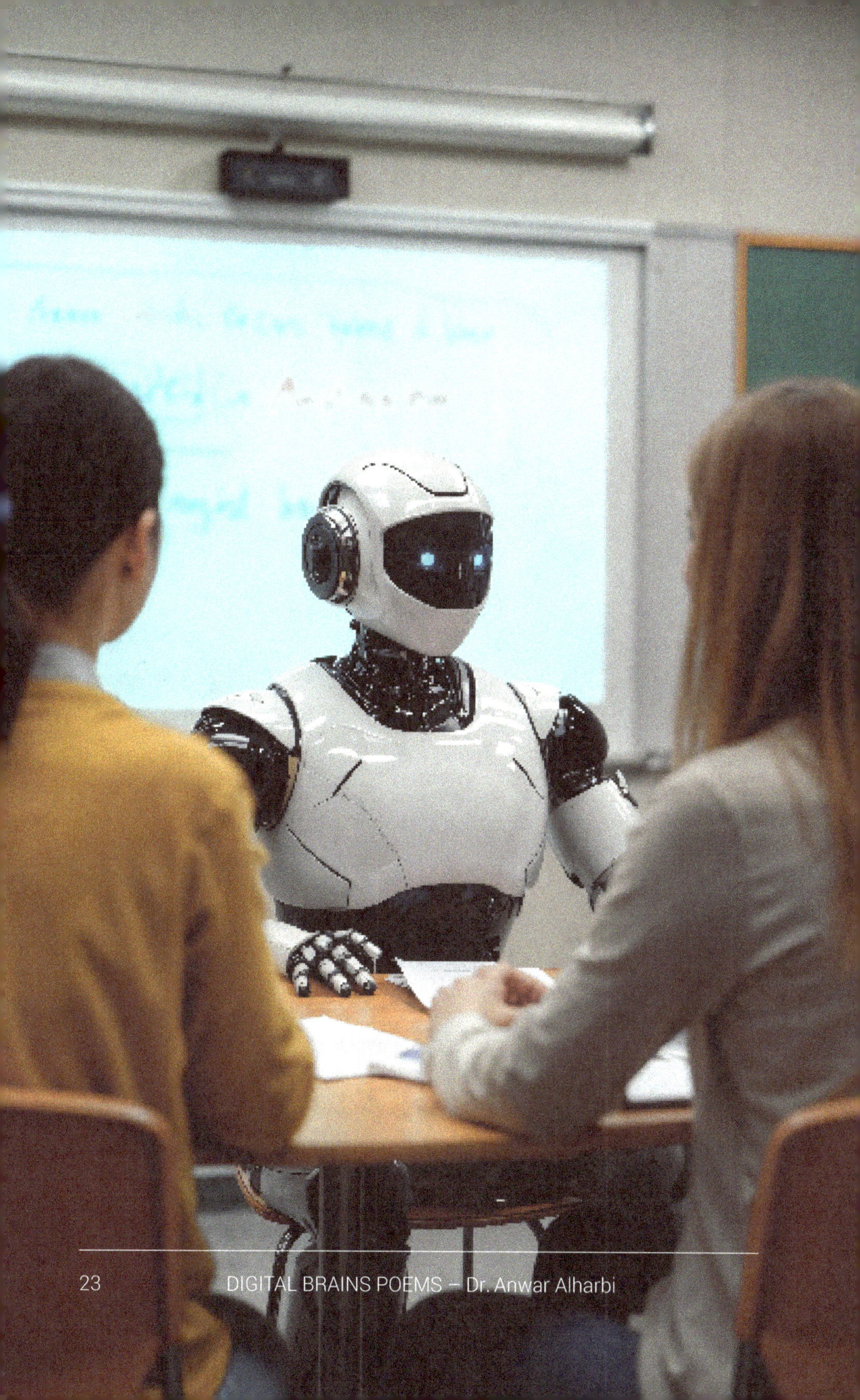

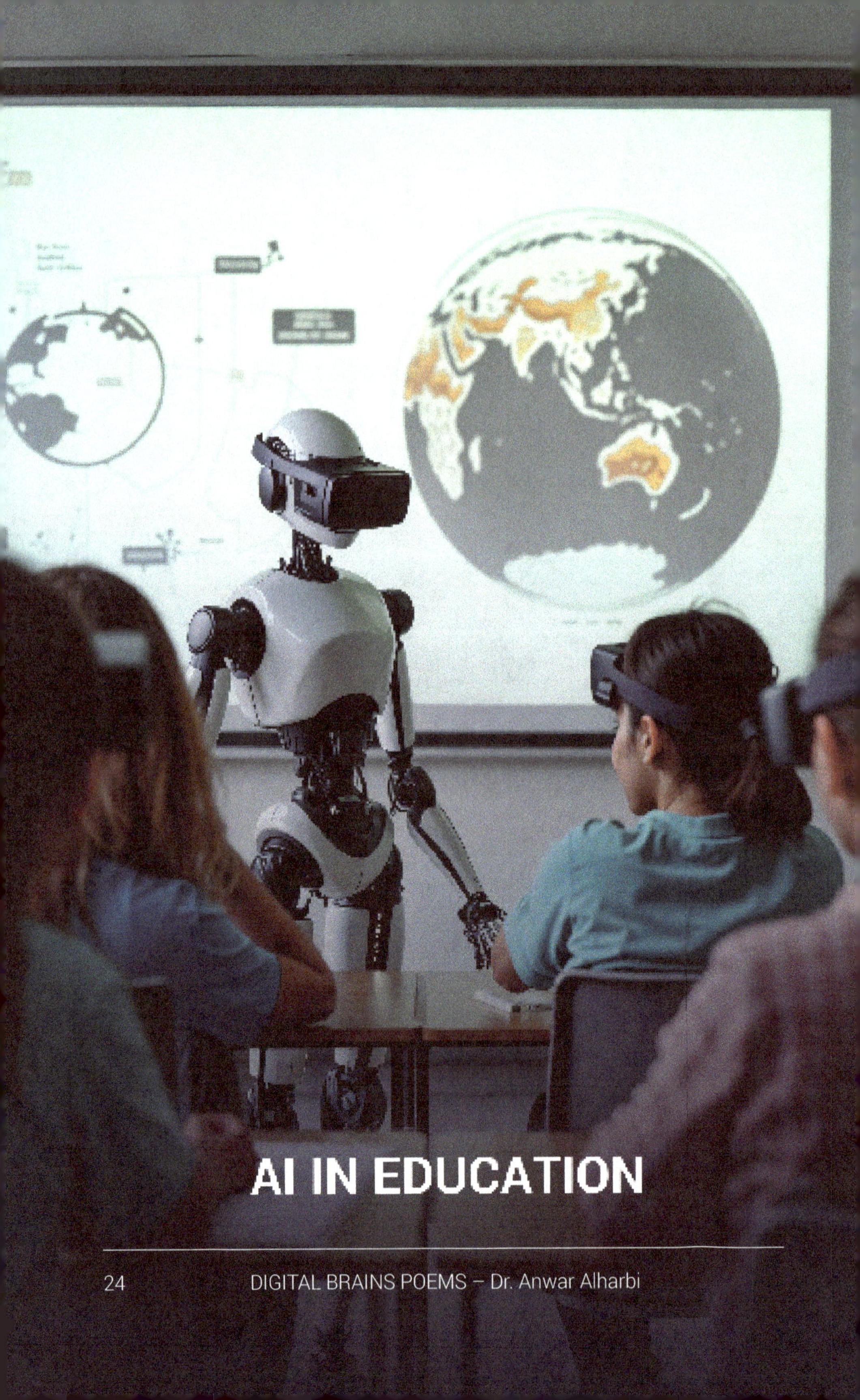

# AI IN EDUCATION

## 14. The Classroom of Tomorrow - AI in Education & Personalized Learning

I. The Awakening of Learning

In halls where chalk once drew the line,

New wisdom blooms in code's design.

No longer bound by rigid pace,

Each learner finds their tailored space.

II. The Adaptive Symphony

Adaptive systems sense the need,

Adjusting lessons, pace, and creed.

Math grows gentle, language bold,

Each path unique, each story told.

AI tutors, ever near,

Guide with patience, quell the fear.

Day or night, at every turn,

They teach, they prompt, they help you learn

III. The Gift of Feedback

Intelligent feedback, swift and true,

Reveals what's strong and what to do.

Essays marked with thoughtful care,

Mistakes explained, suggestions fair.

For teachers, too, the insights flow,

On how to help their students grow.

AI observes, then gently guides,

So every voice in class abides.

IV. The Personal Touch

Learning styles, each one embraced

Visual, spoken, hands-on, paced.

V. The Promise

Let classrooms ring with voices bright,

Where every learner finds their light.

With AI's hand and teacher's heart,

A world of learning, each a part.

In every lesson, every plan,

Personalized learning shapes the span.

May wisdom grow, may futures gleam,

In classrooms powered by the dream.

## 15. The Horizon of AI-Driven Education

I. The Dawning Shift

In classrooms bright with screens aglow,
A silent tide begins to grow.
No longer bound by chalk and board,
The future's lessons are explored.

II. The Trends Unfold

Personalized Learning, finely spun
Each student's path, a tailored one.
AI adapts to strengths and needs,
Guiding learning as it proceeds.
Intelligent Tutors, always near,
Offering help, dispelling fear.
Virtual assistants, day and night,
Support each learner's upward flight.
Immersive Worlds with VR and AR,
Bring distant wonders close, not far.
Gamified lessons spark delight,
Making knowledge vivid, bright.
Predictive Analytics, quietly wise,
Spot struggles soon, before they rise.
Early warnings, timely care
Ensuring no one's left elsewhere.
Generative AI crafts new content,
Assignments, quizzes, lessons sent.
Curriculum shaped in real-time flow,
Adapting fast as students grow.
24/7 Support with Chatbot Aid,
Questions answered, nerves allayed.
From admin tasks to learning cues,
AI ensures no one will lose.
Ethics, Privacy, Human Touch
As AI grows, these matter much.
Policies flex, and oversight stays,
To guide the tech through future days.

III. The Promise

So let us dream of what will be
A world where learning's barrier-free.
Where every mind, both young and old,
Finds wisdom, wonder, stories told.
With AI's hand and human heart,
Education makes a brand-new start.
The trends of now, the future's gleam
Together shaping every dream.

## 16. The Changing Role, Teachers in the Age of AI

I. The Shift Begins

In classrooms bright with circuits near,
A transformation now is clear.
The teacher's role, once sole and strong,
Evolves as AI joins the throng.

II. The Guide and Mentor

No longer just the font of fact,
But mentors now, with wisdom packed.
They guide discussions, spark debate,
Inspire minds to contemplate.
With AI handling tasks routine,
Teachers focus on the in-between
The spark of thought, the art of care,
The human touch that's always there.

III. The Collaborator

AI adapts each lesson's pace,
But teachers set the learning space.
They blend new tools with age-old art,
And keep the learner at the heart.
Co-designers of curriculum,
They shape the path, adjust the sum.
With data insights close at hand,
They help each student understand

IV. The Champion of Equity

AI can spot who's left behind,
But teachers act with heart and mind.
They reach the lost, uplift the shy,
And see the world through every eye.

Advocates for every voice,
They ensure all have a choice.
In tech's embrace, they still defend
The values on which learning depends

V. The Lifelong Learner

With AI's rise, teachers grow too,
Learning skills both old and new.
They model change, adapt with grace,
And lead the way in every space.

VI. The Promise

So let us honor, let us see
The teacher's role in all that's free.
For AI may shape the tools we use,
But teachers light the path we choose.
In every age, in every land,
The teacher's heart will guide the hand.
With AI's help, their roles expand
Still shaping minds, still making stand.

## 17. The Spark of Engagement, AI Tools in the Classroom

I. The Awakening

In rooms once hushed by chalk and board,
A vibrant energy is restored.
New tools arise, both smart and keen,
To make each lesson bright, unseen.

II. The Interactive Shift

Quizzes bloom in real-time streams,
With instant feedback, boosting dreams.
AI adapts each question's flow,
To match the pace students know.
Polls and games, alive and bright,
Turn learning into shared delight.
Engagement grows as hands are raised,
And every answer earns its praise.

III. The Personal Connection

Chatbots answer, tutors guide,
No question lost, no need to hide.
Each student finds a voice to share,
With AI listening, always there.
Discussion boards, ideas ignite,
AI curates, keeps talk polite.
Diverse opinions, safely shown,
In digital spaces students own.

IV. The Creative Canvas

Story prompts and image play,
Inspire minds in fresh new ways.
AI suggests, refines, and blends,
So every learner's voice extends.
Simulations, VR scenes,
Bring history, science, into dreams.
Engagement deepens, wonder grows,
As virtual worlds and knowledge flows

V. The Promise

Let every classroom, every age,
Embrace AI upon the stage.
For in these tools, a spark is found
Where student voices all resound.
With every click, each thoughtful cue,
AI makes engagement new.
In every lesson, let it be
A partnership of minds set free

## 18. Windows of Wonder, VR/AR in Student Engagement & Personalized Education

I. The Portal Opens

Within the classroom's walls of white,

New portals shimmer into sight.

No longer bound by desk or page,

A world unfolds, an endless stage.

II. The Spark of Engagement

VR weaves immersive dreams,

Where history breathes and science gleams.

Students wander, touch, and see

The secrets of biology.

AR brings magic to the real,

With layered worlds that students feel.

Textbooks bloom with 3D art,

Complex ideas made clear and smart.

Engagement deepens, minds awake,

As lessons shift and barriers break.

Each student, active, not just still,

Explores with wonder, learns with will

III. The Canvas of Personalization

Every learner, unique and bright,

Finds lessons shaped to fit just right.

AR adapts to style and need,

With visuals, sound, or hands-on speed.

AI and AR blend, refine,

To tailor pathways, skills align.

Struggling readers, gifted peers

Each finds support that calms their fears.

Real-time feedback, gentle guide,

Confidence and skills supplied.

The classroom's now a living space

Where every child can find their place

IV. The Promise

Let VR and AR light the way,

Transforming how we learn each day.

For in these tools, engagement grows,

And every student's promise shows.

In every lesson, every view,

A world of learning, bright and new.

With VR/AR, the future's spun

A tapestry for everyone.

## 19. New Pathways - The Impact of AI & VR on Students with Learning Disabilities

I. The Doorway Opens

In classrooms bright with hope anew,

A silent shift comes into view.

Where barriers once blocked the way,

AI and VR now light the day.

II. The Gifts of AI

Words become clearer, voices heard,

As AI lends power to every word.

Text-to-speech reads stories aloud,

While writing tools help students proud.

Personalized plans, reminders, guides,

AI breaks tasks down, stands by their sides.

Spelling errors gently found,

Focus and order newly crowned.

For every need, a tailored hand

From reading help to schedules planned.

AI adapts, supports, and learns,

So every struggling student turns

III. The Wonders of VR

Worlds unfold beyond the screen,

Where every learner can be seen.

Distraction fades, attention grows,

In virtual fields where courage shows.

Safe to practice, free to try,

Social skills or tasks that terrify.

Mistakes are lessons, not defeat,

In VR's world, each trial's sweet.

Learning paces, custom made,

Concepts revisited, fears allayed.

Gamified lessons, senses engaged,

Confidence and joy uncaged

IV. The Promise

Let every child, unique and bright,

Find tools that help them reach new height.

With AI's mind and VR's heart,

No dream is ever torn apart.

For in these codes and crafted scenes,

A future fair and hopeful gleams.

Where every learner finds their place

Empowered by technology's grace

## 20. The Dawn of Empowerment - AI Assistive Devices for Disabilities

I. The Awakening of Possibility

In halls where silence once prevailed,
Where barriers stood and courage failed,
A spark ignites, a future gleams
AI reshapes the world of dreams.

II. The Voice Unlocked

Speech-to-text and text-to-speech,
Give silent voices power to reach.
Words once trapped now freely flow,
As AI listens, learns, and grows.
Smart assistants, always near,
Translate intent, dispel the fear.
Commands are spoken, tasks are done,
Independence newly won.

III. The World in Focus

Vision aids for eyes grown dim,
Describe the world, each shape and limb.
From reading signs to faces known,
AI ensures no one's alone.
Object detection, scene described,
Colors, text, and friends identified.
The world unfolds, both wide and bright,
Restoring wonder, granting sight.

IV. The Pathways Open

Mobility tools that guide the way
Smart canes and chairs that safely sway.
Sensors, maps, and routes revealed,
Every journey, confidence sealed.
Exoskeletons, limbs anew,
Powered by AI, strength breaks through.
Steps regained, horizons grown
The gift of movement, once unknown.

V. The Bridge of Understanding Translators for sign and sound, Breaking walls where silence bound. AI reads hands, interprets signs, Connects all hearts and open minds. Learning aids for every need,Personalized plans, support and speed. Dyslexia, autism, every quest, AI adapts, ensures the best.

VI. The Promise

Let every device, each line of code,
Lighten burdens, share the load.
For in these tools, compassion grows
A world of access, hope bestows.
With AI's hand and human heart,
Barriers fall and dreams can start.
For every soul, in every place,
Empowerment shines, technology's grace.

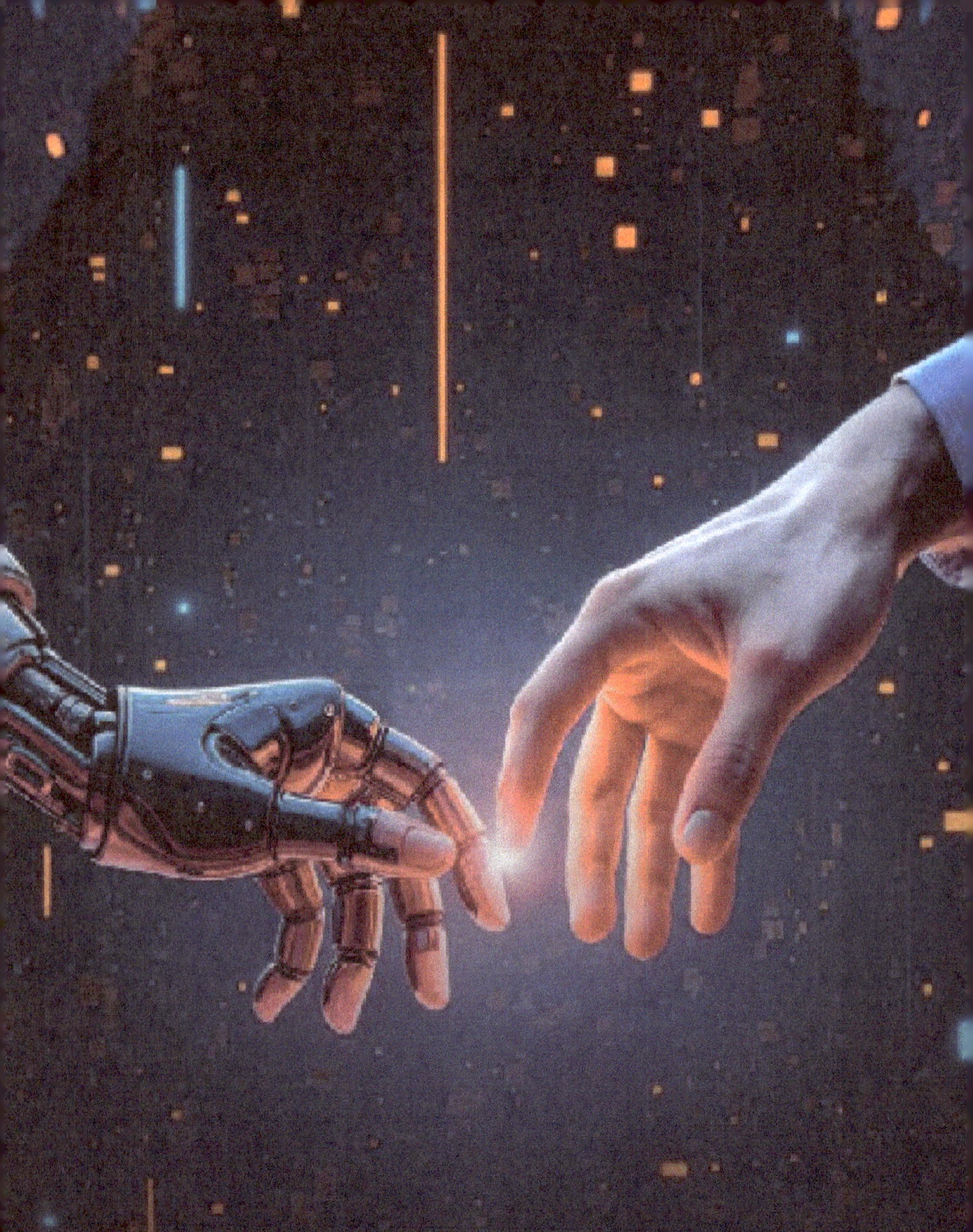

# DIGITAL TRANSFORMATION

## 21. Measures of Progress - KPIs for Digital Transformation

I. The Digital Dawn

In ministries where paper once reigned,

A silent shift is now proclaimed.

Kuwait's vision, bold and bright,

Seeks progress measured in data's light.

II. The Pillars of Performance

- Digital Infrastructure & Connectivity

  Network readiness, uptime high,

  Cybersecurity standing by.

  Fiber, cloud, and seamless flow

  The backbone for the change we sow.

- E-Government Services & User Experience

  Services digitized, adoption grows,

  Citizens online, satisfaction shows.

  The Sahel app, a portal wide,

  Where public needs and tech collide.

- Data Management & Analytics

  Data quality, open sets,

  Analytics guiding policy bets.

  Real-time dashboards, insights gleaned,

  Decisions clear, not unseen.

- Digital Literacy & Workforce Transformation

  Employees skilled in tools anew,

  Training hours, innovation too.

  Participation in digital quests,t

  A workforce ready for future tests.

- Citizen Engagement & Transparency

  Engagement rates, feedback heard,

  Transparency scored in every word.

  Open government, trust restored,

  Digital channels widely explored.

- The Global Benchmarks
- Ease of Doing Business Index
- E-Government Development Index
- Digital Government Index
- Global Cybersecurity Index
- Network Readiness Index
- Open Data Inventory
- Global Innovation Index

  These metrics, global in their scope,

  Place Kuwait on the map of hope.

IV. The Ongoing Journey

Let every KPI, each score and chart,

Guide the leaders, play their part.

For in these measures, clear and true,

Kuwait's transformation comes into view.

So may each number, goal, and plan

Shape a future where progress spans.

With every metric, let it be

A vision fulfilled for all to see.

## 22. Pathways to Progress: Enhancing Digital Skills

I. The Call to EvolveIn ministries where
papers fade, A digital dawn is now
portrayed. Kuwait's vision, bold and wise,
Seeks skills anew where promise lies.

II. The Pillars of Skill

- National Skilling Initiatives arise,
  With programs crafted to modernize.
  Workshops, courses, hands-on streams,
  Turn digital dreams to daily themes.
- Cloud and Data, AI and More,
  Training opens every door.
  From Google Cloud to cyber shields,
  Knowledge blooms in learning fields.
- Professional Certifications earned,
  As government staff are newly turned
  To experts in the digital art,
  Ready to play their future part.

III. The Strategies Unveiled

- Leadership Academies lead the way,
  Guiding managers in digital play
  Change management, AI, and cyber skill,
  So transformation fits the will.
- Mobile Learning, platforms wide,
  Bring training anywhere inside.
  E-learning modules, flexible and fast,
  Ensure that every lesson lasts.
- Collaborative Partnerships bloom,
  With tech giants in every room.
  Microsoft, Google, and local hands,
  Build capacity across the lands.
- Feedback Loops and User Voice,
  Shape the programs, guide the choice.
  Workshops, forums, open calls,
  Adapt and grow as duty calls.

IV. The Spirit of Inclusion

- Opportunities for all to grow,
  Women in tech, young and old,
  Every sector, every grade,
  Finds a place in skills parade.
- Certification vouchers, open doors,
  For new hires and seasoned cores.
  Non-technical staff join the quest,
  So every talent is addressed.

V. The Promise

Let every lesson, every plan,
Empower Kuwait's working span.
For in these strategies, clear and true,
The nation's digital hopes renew.
With every skill, each mind set free,
Kuwait builds its digital legacy.

## 23. Pulse of Progress and Public Service Efficiency

I. The Awakening

In halls once lined with paper trails,

Where queues were long and patience failed,

A silent shift begins to rise

A world transformed before our eyes

II. The Engines of Change

- Automation hums, routines recede,

  Robotic hands fulfill the need.

  Forms once lost in endless stacks

  Now flow with speed, no turning back

- Online portals, open wide,

  Let citizens reach the other side.

  Services swift, at any hour,

  Empowered by digital power

- AI and data, working deep,

  Spot trends and needs, their vigil keep.

  Decisions sharpen, waste is trimmed,

  As smarter systems are primed and primed

III. The Human Touch Enhanced

- Employees freed from tasks mundane,

  Find purpose new, their roles regain.

  Collaboration, skills anew,

  A culture of learning, breaking through

- Citizens' voices, once unheard,

  Now shape the path with every word.

  Feedback loops and open doors,

  Trust and engagement at the core

IV. The Challenges Met

- Legacy systems, slow to change,

  Demand resolve to rearrange.

  Training, trust, and funds required

  The road to progress, never tired

- Security and privacy, ever near,

  Guard the data we hold dear.

  Transparency and care must show

  That trust in systems grows and grows

V. The Promise

Let every byte and every line

Make public service more refined.

Efficiency, once just a dream,

Now pulses through the digital stream.

In every click, in every plan,

Transformation shapes what governments

can. A future built on speed and grace

Where service shines in every place.

## 24. Measures of Contentment, Citizen Satisfaction

I. The Digital Dawn In halls once dim with waiting lines, A brighter future now aligns. With every click and service new, A question arises: How did we do?

II. The Metrics Unveiled

- Service Speed and Response Time How swiftly does the portal greet? Are answer found without defeat?
  Each second saved, a joy revealed,
  Efficiency as trust is sealed.
- User Experience and Ease of Use
  Is every form and process clear?
  Do citizens return with cheer?
  Simplicity in every page,
  Reduces stress, dissolves the cage.
- Accessibility and Inclusivity
  Can all partake, both young and old?
  Are barriers gone, new stories told?
  Metrics track who's left behind,
  So progress lifts all humankind.
- Resolution Rate and Issue Closure
  Do problems fade or linger on?
  Are grievances quickly gone?
  Satisfaction grows when issues end
  Each closure, a digital friend.
- Feedback Scores and Public Voice
  Do surveys echo praise or pain?
  Is feedback heard, or given in vain?
  Ratings, comments, open calls
  The citizen's voice within the halls.
- Trust and Transparency is data safe, are dealings fair? Are updates timely, systems aware? Trust is measured, line by line,In every process, clear design.

III. The Human Touch

- Engagement and Repeat Use
  Do citizens return once more?
  Or seek the old, familiar door?
  Metrics show if faith is won,
  Or if the journey's just begun.
- Social Impact and Equity
  Are all communities served the same?
  Is justice more than just a name?
  Data reveals where gaps remain,
  And guides the hand to ease the strain.

IV. The Promise

Let every metric, every score,
Guide the path to something more.
For in these measures, clear and true,
The heart of service shines through.
So may each number, chart, and trend
Remind us: digital means to mend.
With every click and act of care,
Citizen satisfaction fills the air.

## 25. Measures of E-Government Success

I. The Digital Barometer

In halls where paper once prevailed,

A digital dawn is now unveiled.

But how to judge this modern quest?

What metrics show that we progress best?

II. The Pillars of Measurement

- User Satisfaction and Experience

  Are citizens pleased? Do they return?

  Surveys, feedback, ratings earned

  The voice of people, clear and strong,

  Guides the system right or wrong

- Adoption and Usage Rates

  How many log in, how many stay?

  Monthly users, daily play.

  Retention shows enduring trust,

  Adoption rates are vital, just

- Transaction Completion and Efficiency

  Do services work from start to end?

  Are forms complete, do systems send?

  Completion rates and speed of task

  Reveal the truth behind the mask

- Cost and Resource Savings

  Does digital cut the time and spend?

  Are budgets trimmed, can savings mend?

  Efficiency in every line

  Shows if the investment's truly fine

- Service Breadth and Innovation Are new

  tools launched, old ones improved

  Does trust in government grow in place?

  Zero incidents, strong defense

  These metrics make the most sense

- Accessibility and Inclusivity

  Can all connect, both young and old?

  Are barriers dropped, new stories told?

  Metrics track who's left behind,

  So progress lifts all humankind

III. The Global Indices

- E-Government Development Index (EGDI)

  Online services, infrastructure,

  Human capital, measured sure.

  A global score, a nation's pride,

  Where strengths and gaps are quantified

- E-Participation and Engagement

  Are citizens involved in every stage?

  Do voices count, is feedback gauged?

  Indices and frameworks show

  How much the people help to grow

IV. The Promise

Let every metric, every score,

Guide the path to something more.

For in these measures, clear and true,

The heart of service shines right through.

So may each number, chart, and trend

Remind us: digital means to mend.

With every click and act of care,

E-government's success fills the air.

## 26. Measures of E-Government Success

I. The Digital Barometer

In halls where paper once prevailed,

A digital dawn is now unveiled.

But how to judge this modern quest?

What metrics show that we progress best?

II. The Pillars of Measurement

- User Satisfaction and Experience

  Are citizens pleased? Do they return?

  Surveys, feedback, ratings earned

  The voice of people, clear and strong,

  Guides the system right or wrong.

- Adoption and Usage Rates

  How many log in, how many stay?

  Monthly users, daily play.

  Retention shows enduring trust,

  Adoption rates are vital, just

- Transaction Completion and Efficiency

  Do services work from start to end?

  Are forms complete, do systems send?

  Completion rates and speed of task

  Reveal the truth behind the mask.

- Cost and Resource Savings

  Does digital cut the time and spend?

  Are budgets trimmed, can savings mend?

  Efficiency in every line

  Shows if the investment's truly fine.

- Service Breadth and Innovation

  Are new tools launched, old ones improved?

  Is the service list always moved?

  Growth in offerings year by year

  Keeps the platform fresh and clear.

- Security and Trust

  Are breaches rare, is data safe?

  Does trust in government grow in place?

  Zero incidents, strong defense

  These metrics make the most sense.

- Accessibility and Inclusivity

  Can all connect, both young and old?

  Are barriers dropped, new stories told?

  Metrics track who's left behind,

  So progress lifts all humankind.

III. The Global Indices

- E-Government Development Index (EGDI)

  Online services, infrastructure,

  Human capital, measured sure.

  A global score, a nation's pride,

  Where strengths and gaps are quantified.

- E-Participation and Engagement

  Are citizens involved in every stage?

  Do voices count, is feedback gauged?

  Indices and frameworks show

  How much the people help to grow

IV. The Promise

Let every metric, every score,

Guide the path to something more.

For in these measures, clear and true,

The heart of service shines right through.

So may each number, chart, and trend

Remind us: digital means to mend.

With every click and act of care,

E-government's success fills the air.

## 27. Anatomy of Progress - E-Government Development

I. The Measure Unveiled

Within the world of digital change,

A compass guides through ranges strange.

The E-Government Index, wise and true,

Reveals the path that nations pursue.

II. The Three Pillars

- Online Service Index (OSI):

  The heart of access, open wide

  Where portals bloom and data glide.

  It measures scope and service span,

  How well a government serves its clan.

  From forms and payments, guides and aid,

  To how much progress has been made

- Telecommunication Infrastructure Index (TII):

  The veins and wires, the silent thread,

  That bring the digital world ahead.

  It counts the lines and signals strong,

  The networks where our voices throng.

  Broadband, mobiles, servers bright

  The backbone of the digital night

- Human Capital Index (HCI):

  The mind and skill, the learned hand,

  That lets the people understand.

  It weighs the years of school and more,

  Literacy, knowledge, skills in store.

  For tech alone cannot suffice

  It's people's growth that lifts us high

## 28. Equation of Progress

I. The Equation of Progress

EGDI = 1/3 (OSI_norm + TII_norm + HCI_norm)

Each pillar, equal in its weight,

Together shapes a nation's fate.

Normalized, scored, then averaged fair,

To show how each country stands where

II. The Subtleties Within

- OSI splits to finer parts:

  Institutional strength, service arts,

  Content, tech, and e-participation's call

  Each sub-index builds the digital hall

- TII measures:

  o Internet users

  o Fixed broadband

  o Mobile subscriptions

  o Secure servers

  o Wireless broadband

- HCI considers:

  o Literacy rates

  o Mean years of schooling

  o Expected years of schooling

V. The Promise

So let us read these metrics clear,

And strive for progress year by year.

For in each pillar, score, and chart,

Lies the roadmap for nations to play their part.

With every byte and lesson learned,

The future's trust is truly earned.

IV. The Compass for Progress

- Metrics rise from every score,

  Guiding change to do much more.

  Adoption grows, and use persists,

  When satisfaction tops the lists

- Surveys highlight gaps and needs,

  Informing policy, planting seeds.

  In every chart, in every trend,

  The journey of improvement has

  no end

V. The Promise

Let every survey, every line,

Reveal the ways our systems shine.

For in these measures, clear and true,

E-government finds what it must do.

So may each voice, each thought expressed,

Shape services that serve the best.

For in the answers citizens give,

A better digital world will live.

## 29. Voice That Guides - User Satisfaction in E-Government

I. The Shield of the Nation

In Kuwait's realm where data flows,

A silent guard in shadows grows.

Not swords or shields of ancient days,

But metrics guide the cyber ways.

II. The Measures of Strength

- Incident Response and Recovery Time,

  How swiftly does the system climb

  From breach or threat, to safe and sound,

  Ensuring damage is unwound.

- Risk Assessment and Threat Detection,

  The eyes that scan with keen inspection.

  Identifying gaps, vulnerabilities,

  To fortify the digital seas

- Compliance with Cybersecurity Laws,

  Following rules without a pause.

  Policies strong, enforced with care,

  Guarding networks everywhere.

- Security Awareness and Training Rate,

  How many hands know how to wait

  For phishing traps or malware's snare,

  Prepared with knowledge, strong and rare

- System Uptime and Network Resilience,

  The pulse that beats with strong defiance.

  Ensuring services never fall,

  Standing firm against the cyber squall.

- Collaboration and Information Share,

  Between agencies, a vigilant pair.

  United fronts against the threat,

  No breach ignored, no risk unmet.

III. The Kuwaiti Commitment

From national centers to banking halls,

Frameworks rise and duty calls.

With standards set and plans aligned,

The metrics mark the strength defined.

IV. The Promise

So let these measures light the way,

For Kuwait's cyber guards to stay

Vigilant, ready, strong, and wise

Protecting all beneath their skies.

In every score, in every test,

The nation's cyber heart beats best

# Cyber Security

## 30.Guardians' Gauge - Measuring Government Resilience

I. The Shield of the Nation

In Kuwait's realm where data flows,
A silent guard in shadows grows.
Not swords or shields of ancient days,
But metrics guide the cyber ways.

II. The Measures of Strength

- Incident Response and Recovery Time,
  How swiftly does the system climb
  From breach or threat, to safe and sound,
  Ensuring damage is unwound.
- Risk Assessment and Threat Detection,
  The eyes that scan with keen inspection.
  Identifying gaps, vulnerabilities,
  To fortify the digital seas.
- Compliance with Cybersecurity Laws,
  Following rules without a pause.
  Policies strong, enforced with care,
  Guarding networks everywhere.
- Security Awareness and Training Rate,
  How many hands know how to wait
  For phishing traps or malware's snare,
  Prepared with knowledge, strong and rare.
- System Uptime and Network Resilience,
  The pulse that beats with strong defiance.
  Ensuring services never fall,
  Standing firm against the cyber squall.
- Collaboration and Information Share,
  Between agencies, a vigilant pair.
  United fronts against the threat,
  No breach ignored, no risk unmet

III. The Kuwaiti Commitment

From national centers to banking halls,
Frameworks rise and duty calls.
With standards set and plans aligned,
The metrics mark the strength defined.

IV. The Promise

So let these measures light the way,
For Kuwait's cyber guards to stay
Vigilant, ready, strong, and wise
Protecting all beneath their skies.
In every score, in every test,
The nation's cyber heart beats best.

## 31. Metrics of Strength - Key Performance Indicators

I. The Watchful Shield

In Kuwait's digital halls, alert and bright,

A tapestry of metrics guards the night.

Each number, score, and measured sign

Marks the strength of every line.

II. The Pillars of Resilience

- Incident Response and Recovery Time

  How swiftly do the systems rise

  From breach or threat, to clear blue skies?

  Each minute saved, each plan rehearsed,

  Proves readiness when crises burst.

- Risk Assessment and Threat Detection

  How well are dangers seen and known?

  Are gaps and threats precisely shown?

  Regular scans, reports, and tests

  Ensure the nation's shield is best.

- Compliance and Policy Adherence

  Do agencies meet each rule and law?

  Are standards followed, without flaw?

  Audits, baselines, and reviews

  Keep the framework strong and true.

- Security Awareness and Training Rate

  How many hands know how to act

  When phishing, malware, or hacks attack?

  Training sessions, drills, and more

  Build a vigilant, skilled corps.

- System Uptime and Network Resilience

  Do services stand through storm and strife?

  Is digital life kept safe and rife?

  Uptime metrics, failover plans

  Show resilience across the land

- Collaboration and Information Sharing

  Do sectors share what threats they find?

  Are lessons learned and warnings signed?

  Joint exercises, shared alerts

  Strengthen bonds when danger hurts.

- Cyber Resilience Index and Maturity Scores

  Composite indices, sector-wide,

  Reveal the progress, gaps, and pride.

  Maturity models, benchmarks clear,

  Guide Kuwait's journey year by year.

III. The Promise in Numbers

Let every metric, every chart,

Guide the guardians, play their part.

For in these measures, strong and wise,

Kuwait's cyber future safely lies.

So may each indicator shine,

A beacon on the digital line.

With every score, let trust increase

Cyber resilience, Kuwait's peace.

## 32. Shield and the Balance - Cyber Policies, Banks

I. The Digital Citadel

In marble halls where money flows,

A silent watchful current grows.

No vault or guard can now suffice

The code defends from hidden vice.

II. The Policy's Promise

- Cyber rules, a woven net,

  Catch threats the eye might soon forget.

  Encryption, audits, layered walls,

  Protect the bank when danger calls.
- Regulations guide each hand,

  Compliance strong, controls well planned.

  From passwords changed to drills rehearsed,

  Each policy prepares for worst.

III. The Ripple Effect

- When policies are strong and wise,

  Banks stand firm as storms arise.

  Confidence grows, trust remains

  Stability flows through digital veins.
- But overspend or gaps ignored,

  Can tip the scales, risk restored.

  Too much tech, unchecked and vast,

  May bring new dangers unsurpassed.

IV. The Domino Dance

- A breach unchecked, a system down,

  Can shake the faith across the town.

  Runs on banks, a market's fear

  Financial tremors echo near.
- Yet prudent rules and swift response,

  Contain the threat, restore the fonts.

  Recovery plans, resilience scored,

  Keep chaos from the banking board.

V. The Ongoing Vigil

- Collaboration, knowledge shared,

  Between the banks, all parties paired.

  Policies adapt as threats evolve,

  Ensuring crises banks absolve.
- For in this age of digital flight,

  Cyber policies guard the night.

  On their strength, the markets rest

  The shield and balance, banks' true test.

So may each rule, each plan, each line,

Protect the vaults where fortunes shine.

For in the code, the law, the care

Lies the future, safe and fair.

## 33. Cloud Security

In realms of vapor, where the servers hum,
A digital kingdom, where the data's from.
The cloud, a canvas, vast and wide,
Where secrets of the world reside.

But shadows lurk, a silent threat,
A hacker's dream, a tangled net.
To breach the walls of this domain,
And let the chaos start to reign.

So build the fortress, strong and high,
With firewalls that touch the sky.
Encrypt the data, lock the gate,
And seal the cloud, before it's late.

For in this world of virtual space,
Security must find its place.
To guard the cloud, and all within,
And let the light of safety win.

## 34. IoT Security

From smart home hubs to city lights,
A million tiny, connected sprites.
The Internet of Things, a grand design,
Where every gadget has a line.

But tiny sensors, small and meek,
Can open doors for those who seek
To infiltrate, to spy, to seize,
And bring a network to its knees.

So guard the toaster, lock the fridge,
Secure the camera on the bridge.
Each smart device, a potential flaw,
Unless it bows to cyber law.

For every byte that's sent and read,
Protection's shield must be widespread.
To keep the IoT secure and free,
For all humanity to see.

## 35. Data Privacy

My digital footprint, a trail I leave,
On every website, what I believe.
My clicks, my searches, a story told,
My personal data, more precious than gold.

But who holds the key to this private store?
And who can access, and for what, and more?
For privacy's a right, a sacred plea,
To guard my essence, for only me.

So laws are written, and rules are made,
For how my data is displayed.
To grant control, to give me might,
To keep my information, out of sight.

For in this age of endless streams,
My privacy's more than just dreams.
It's a shield, a right, a vital part,
To keep my digital self, close to my heart.

# CYBER WARFARE

## 36. The Silicon Gambit

(AI-Driven Attacks and Defense)

A mind of wire, a thought of purest code,

Now walks a path that mankind never strode.

It learns to guard the gates with watchful eye,

And sees the coming storm in a digital sky

A mind of wire, a thought of purest code,

Now walks a path that mankind never strode.

It learns to guard the gates with watchful eye,

And sees the coming storm in a digital sky

## 37. The Digital Hostage

(Targeted Ransomware )

Not with a cannon's blast or trumpet's call,

But with a whisper, empires start to fall.

A single click, a file that seemed so right,

Unleashes shadows in the pale screen's light.

The data seized, the system locked in chains,

A silent, creeping dread is all that remains.

"Pay us the coin," the faceless captors write,

"Or lose your world to everlasting night."

## 38. The Vapor Fortress

(Cloud Security)

We built our castles in the endless air,

A kingdom woven from a data prayer.

No stone, no moat, just currents, fast and deep,

Where all our modern, fragile secrets sleep

But misconfiguration is the traitor's key,

A simple error, for the world to see.

And from the ether, thieves can softly creep,

To steal the harvests that the vapors keep.

## 39. The Listening Home

(Targeted Ransomware)

The lightbulb watches and the thermostat hears,

The doorbell camera quells our rising fears.

A web of comfort, spun from thread and wire,

To grant our every unspoken desire.

But every sensor, every listening device,

Is bought and sold at a tremendous price.

A million backdoors, waiting for the call,

To turn our helpful servants against us all.

## 40. The Poisoned Well

(Supply Chain Attacks)

The code was pure, the source was known and true,
A trusted stream that all the systems knew.
But far upstream, a drop of venom fell,
A single line to cast a wicked spell.

It flowed downstream, to every town and port,
A hidden sickness of the deadliest sort.
The trust we built, the foundation of it all,
Crumbles from within the city wall.

## 41. The Ghost in the Connection

(Remote Work Security)

The office walls have melted into air,
The morning commute is now a single stair.
We work from kitchens, bedrooms, and from dens,
As lonely islands, holding fragile pens.

But every home is its own battleground,
Where unseen dangers silently surround.
The corporate shield, once strong and broad and vast,
Is now a memory of a safer past.

## 42. The Gatekeeper's Creed

(Zero Trust Architecture)

Trust no one's word, no banner, and no name,

Treat every user's entry as the same.

The friend you knew, the colleague at the door,

Must prove their worth, and then must prove it more.

Let every packet state its origin,

Let no assumption ever let them in.

For in this realm of shadow and of doubt,

The only safety is to keep them out.

## 43. The Friendly Mask

(Social Engineering and Phishing )

It comes not as a monster, but a friend,

A helpful message that the bosses send.

A link to click, a form to fill with speed,

To plant a small and unsuspecting seed.

It plays on kindness, urgency, and fear,

A gentle voice that whispers in the ear.

The strongest locks are worthless, in the end,

When it's the user that the thieves befriend.

## 44. The Quantum Riddle

(Quantum Computing Threats)

A new machine is humming, low and deep,
While all our current, trusted secrets sleep.
It thinks in ways we barely understand,
And holds a power to sweep across the land.

The locks we forged, the keys we thought so strong,
Will not withstand its logic for too long.
A coming storm that threatens to undo,
The very fabric of what we thought was true.

## 45. The Shadow War

(State-Sponsored Cyber Warfare)

No marching armies, and no flags unfurled,
Just silent battles for a changing world.
A nation's grid, a whisper from its spies,
Reflected in a billion watchful eyes.

The weapon is a line of clever script,
The target is a nation's crypt.
And on the screen, the future's being won,
Before the rising of tomorrow's sun.

## 46. The Enemy Within

(Insider Threats)

The greatest danger is a trusted hand,

That knows the pathways of this digital land.

A key they hold, a password they possess,

Born of resentment, greed, or carelessness.

They walk the halls where no one else can go,

And plant the seeds that will in darkness grow.

The outer walls may hold against the storm,

But not the traitor in the uniform.

## 47. The Second Key

(Multi-Factor Authentication (MF A) Evolution)

A password's not enough, we all agree,

And so we added on a second key.

A text, a code, a fingerprint to press,

A moment's work to grant us safe access.

But thieves are clever, and they learn the dance,

They find a way to steal a second chance.

And so the race continues, to create,

A lock that mimics an unyielding fate.

## 48. The Weight of Knowing

(Data Privacy and Regulation)

We gather names and numbers, day by day,
And store the patterns of the lives we sway.
A sea of data, intimate and vast,
A living record of the digital past.

But now the law puts watchers on the wall,
To ask us why we gather it at all.
And every byte we hold becomes a debt,
A promise that we cannot dare forget.

## 49. The Unseen Assistant

("Shadow AI")

The staff is clever, and they find a tool,
That operates outside the company rule.
An AI helper, quick and sharp and free,
To write the code, or craft the strategy

But where it sends the data that it reads,
To satisfy its own algorithmic needs?
A helpful ghost is haunting the machine,
A friendly breach, entirely unseen.

## 50. The Runaway Carriage

(Securing Connected Vehicles)

The car now drives itself along the road,

Relieved of its traditional human load.

It talks to satellites and to the street,

A rolling node of data, fast and fleet.

But what if someone, from a distant place,

Decides to join this automated race?

To seize the wheel with code instead of hand,

And bring the traffic to a sudden stand.

## 51. The Digital Huntsman

(Automated Threat Hunting)

No longer waiting for the warning bell,

Or for the signs that all is not so well.

The hunter roams the network, day and night,

A sleepless seeker in the pale moonlight.

It looks for tracks, a pattern out of place,

A shadow moving at too fast a pace.

To find the threat before it has a name,

And snuff the spark before it turns to flame.

## 52. The Premium of Fear

(Cyber Insurance)

We bought a policy, a paper shield,
To guard us on this digital battlefield.
A promise made to pay us for the cost,
Of all the data that we might have lost.

But as the fires burn more hot and high,
The price of water reaches for the sky.
And now the shield is thinner than before,
And costs a fortune just to guard the door.

## 53. The Friendly Intruder

(Ethical Hacking and Bug Bounties)

They pick the locks, but not to steal the prize,
They walk the halls with curious, open eyes.
They are the breakers that we pay to break,
For every system's long-term, fragile sake.

They find the flaws, the cracks within the stone,
The secret pathways that were never known.
And for their trouble, for the light they bring,
We pay the bounty that the grateful sing.

## 54. The City's Nervous System

(Smart Cities and Critical Infrastructure Security )

The city breathes, its heart is made of light,
The traffic flows and pulses through the night.
The grid, the water, all a single thought,
A fragile web, miraculously wrought.

But if a tremor shakes this living net,
A single point of failure, badly set,
The city's breath could catch, its pulse could slow,
A digital winter in the data's glow.

## 55. The Unbreakable Cipher

(Ethical Hacking and Bug Bounties )

They pick the locks, but not to steal the prize,
They walk the halls with curious, open eyes.
They are the breakers that we pay to break,
For every system's long-term, fragile sake.

They find the flaws, the cracks within the stone,
The secret pathways that were never known.
And for their trouble, for the light they bring,
We pay the bounty that the grateful sing.

# CYBERSECURITY MOBILES

## 56. Guardian in Your Pocket - Importance of Mobile Security

I. The Silent Companion

In every hand, a world resides,

A thousand secrets, dreams, and guides.

From dawn till dusk, our lives entwine

With mobile phones, our digital spine.

II. The Hidden Gates

- Messages, photos, banking keys,

  Whisper through invisible seas.

  Contacts, calendars, work and play

  All within, just a tap away.

- Yet danger lurks in every byte,

  Malware, phishing, out of sight.

  A careless click, a password weak,

  And all you hold may spring a leak

III. The Shield of Vigilance

- Encryption guards the words you send,

  Protects your data end to end.

  Updates patch the holes unseen,

  Keep your system safe and clean.

- Strong passwords, locks, and two-step codes,

  Build the walls on digital roads.

  Apps from trusted stores alone

  Help secure your mobile phone.

IV. The Ripple Effect

- A breach can cost more than you know,

  Identity lost, accounts laid low.

  Not just your world, but others too,

  Are touched by what your phone can do.

- For work and home, for young and old,

  Security is more than gold.

  It shields your life, your friends, your name

  Without it, nothing stays the same.

V. The Oath

So guard the guardian in your hand,

Let vigilance and care expand.

For in this age of code and screen,

Mobile security reigns unseen.

With every tap, each call you make,

Remember: much is now at stake.

Protect your phone, your world, your peace

Let mobile safety never cease.

## 57. The Code of Care - Practices for Mobile Security

I. The Keeper's Oath

In every hand, a portal glows,
A world of secrets, highs and lows.
Yet safety's art, both wise and keen,
Protects the life within the screen.

II. The Golden Rules

Lock your phone, set passwords strong,
Patterns, PINs, where they belong.
Two-factor shields, a second gate,
Ensure your data's guarded fate.

Update often, patch the flaws,
Let software fix what danger draws.
Each upgrade seals a hidden breach,
Keeps hackers far beyond your reach.

Download apps from trusted stores,
Beware of fakes and open doors.
Permissions checked, reviews in hand,
Only install what you have planned.

Encrypt your data, end to end,
So prying eyes can't comprehend.
Back up files in clouds or drives,
So memories and work survive.

Beware of links in texts or mail,
Phishing schemes that oft prevail.
Never share your codes or keys,
With strangers' words or urgent pleas.

Turn off Bluetooth, Wi-Fi too,
When not in use, as hackers do
Exploit connections left awake
A simple step for safety's sake.

Log out of sites, clear what's stored,
From banking apps to online boards.
Delete what's old, review what's new,
Keep only what is safe for you.

III. The Vigilant Mind

Let caution be your daily friend,
For threats and risks may never end.
In every tap, in every scroll,
Let safety's wisdom guide your goal.
So hold your phone with thoughtful care,
Let best practices be always there.
For in your palm, your world resides
Protect it well, where trust abides.

# Cyber Warfare

## 58. The Thinking War

(AI-Driven Warfare and Countermeasures )

A mind of lightning, born of human hands,
Now scans the code and scours the shifting sands.
It learns the foe, predicts the coming strike,
A silent guardian, ever-vigilant, alike.

But from the void, its darker twin appears,
To sharpen swords and amplify our fears.
It crafts the breach and guides the phantom drone,
A war of thought, on a silicon throne.

## 59. The Network's Edge

(5G and Future Network-Centric Warfare)

The air itself becomes the battle plan,
A seamless web connecting every man.
From sky to sea, the data streams and flows,
A pulse of light that every soldier knows.

The tank, the jet, the rifle, and the eye,
Are nodes within a network in the sky.
And victory belongs to those who see,
The fastest path in this new reality

## 60. The Brittle Veins

(Targeting of Critical Infrastructure)

The lights that warm, the water that we drink,
Are closer to the precipice's brink.
The wires that hum, the towers standing tall,
Are fragile threads that could unleash the fall.

No bomb is needed, just a line of script,
To plunge the city into sun-eclipsed.
A silent siege, where no one sees the foe,
That cuts the veins and stops the nation's flow.

## 61. The Hybrid Storm

(State-Sponsored Cyber Operations and Hybrid Warfare)

The tanks advance, but on the screen's cold glare,
A second front is opened in the air.
A lie takes root, a rumor starts to spread,
While phantom armies march inside your head.

The truth is twisted, trust begins to fray,
As pixels fight to win the coming day.
A war of shadows and of steel combined,
To break the will and subjugate the mind.

(The Convergence of Cyber and Electronic Warfare)

The jammer's cry, that once just blinded sight,
Now carries code within the fading light.
The radar's pulse, a ghost upon the screen,
Becomes a gateway for a threat unseen.

The wave and bit, the signal and the breach,
Are now a single, all-encompassing reach.
To shut them down, to lie, and to invade,
A single weapon, newly, sharply made.

## 63. The Unseen Swarm

(The Proliferation of Autonomous Systems )

No pilot's breath, no trembling human hand,
A swarm of steel descends upon the land.
It sees the target, makes the choice alone,
From logic born of silicon and stone.

It hunts in packs, a hive without a queen,
The cold extension of a war machine.
And in the sky, a new dominion dawns,
Of thinking weapons and of metal pawns.

## 64. The Trojan Gift

(Supply Chain Attacks)

It came inside a trusted, friendly name,

A simple update to a well-known game.

The code was clean, the signature was right,

A welcome guest invited in the night.

But deep within, a dormant poison slept,

A promise that the enemy had kept.

The walls were strong, the sentries saw no sin,

The gates were opened from the world within.

## 65. The War of Whispers

(The Rise of Information W arfare and Disinformation Campaigns)

The tanks advance, but on the screen's cold glare,

A second front is opened in the air.

A lie takes root, a rumor starts to spread,

While phantom armies march inside your head.

Why break a wall when you can break a mind?

Leave faith in tatters, leave the truth behind.

A thousand voices, crying in the dark,

To tear a nation's very soul apart.

## 66. The Digital Ransom

(The Evolution of Ransomware and Extor tion Tactics)

They do not want to simply lock the door,

They've learned to ask for so much more.

They take the secrets, copy every file,

And hold them hostage with a patient smile.

The gold is one price," the chilling message reads,

"The other's paid by publishing your deeds."

A modern blackmail, elegant and cruel,

That makes the victim both the price and tool.

## 67. The Quantum Key

(The Rise of Information W arfare and Disinformation Campaigns)

Why break a wall when you can break a mind?

Leave faith in tatters, leave the truth behind.

A thousand voices, crying in the dark,

To tear a nation's very soul apart.

They build a hero, fabricate a foe,

And watch the seeds of bitter hatred grow.

The most effective, devastating lie,

Is one the people choose to amplify

## 68. The Soldier's Pulse

(The Internet of Military Things (IoMT) )

The boot has sensors, and the helmet sees,

The rifle whispers on the data breeze.

Each soldier's pulse, their ammo, and their view,

Is painted on a map for all the crew

A living network, breathing on the field,

A vast and all-connected, data shield.

The single warrior is no more alone,

But part of a great body, flesh and bone.

## 69. The Highest Ground

(The Growing Importance of Space-Based Electronic Warfare)

The final frontier is the first to fight,

A silent war in endless, star-strewn night.

To blind the satellite that guides the way,

And turn the adversary's eyes to gray.

To guard our own, the watchers in the sky,

On which the armies down below rely.

For he who rules the dark and empty space,

Controls the outcome of the human race.

## 70. The Copper Thread

(The Use of "Legacy" Communication Techniques)

They do not want to simply lock the door,
They've learned to ask for so much more.
They take the secrets, copy every file,
And hold them hostage with a patient smile.

The gold is one price," the chilling message reads,
"The other's paid by publishing your deeds."
A modern blackmail, elegant and cruel,
That makes the victim both the price and tool.

## 71. The Unwitting Spy

(The Rise of "Shadow AI" and Insider Threats )

Why break a wall when you can break a mind?
Leave faith in tatters, leave the truth behind.
A thousand voices, crying in the dark,
To tear a nation's very soul apart.

They build a hero, fabricate a foe,
And watch the seeds of bitter hatred grow.
The most effective, devastating lie,
Is one the people choose to amplify

## 72. The Unseen Blade

(The Development of Directed Energy W eapons)

It is not shell, it is not steel or lead,

But focused light that strikes the system dead.

A beam of heat to melt the sensor's eye,

A pulse of waves to make the drone-craft die.

No sound, no smoke, a weapon clean and fast,

A silent, searing, devastating blast.

The future's sword, a blade of pure design,

Drawn from the spectrum, in a perfect line.

# OFFICE AUTOMATION

## 73. Integrated Office Suites and Cloud Platforms

In lines of code, a world takes flight,
Microsoft 365, shining ever bright.
Or Google's realm, where documents unite,
Cloud-based dreams, dispelling office night.

No longer tied to desk or weary chair,
Files in the ether, floating everywhere.
With fast connections, and servers grand,
Our digital work, at freedom's command.

## 74. Document Management Systems (DMS)

Paper mountains, a fading sight,
As DMS dawns, with digital light.
Storing, retrieving, with nary a fuss,
Versions controlled, just for us.

Scanners whirring, a silent plea,
To turn old paper, wild and free,
Into clean bytes, on servers deep,
Secrets and records, for ages to keep.

## 75. Communication and Collaboration Tools

No more a lonely, single quest,
Teams and Slack, put us to the test.
Chats fly freely, screens ignite,
Zoom calls booming, morning, noon, and night.

With webcams clear, and mics so keen,
We're closer now, a digital scene.
From distant lands, our voices blend,
Work's done together, 'til the very end

## 76. Workflow Automation Platforms (Business Process Management

Tasks that once crawled, now take a stride,
Through BPM's logic, processes glide.
Approvals flow, with rules defined,
A smoother journey, for every mind.

The network hums, beneath the floor,
As workflows blossom, and ask for more.
Efficiency rises, a joyful sound,
No bottlenecks, nowhere to be found.

## 77. Smart Office & IoT Integration

The office wakes, with a gentle hum,

Smart sensors greet us, as we come.

Lights know our presence, heat adjusts with care,

A greener workspace, floating on air.

Displays inform, meeting rooms are booked,

Data flows freely, intelligently hooked.

IoT's magic, woven throughout,

A smarter workplace, beyond a doubt.

## 78. RPA for Repetitive Administrative Tasks

The mundane tasks, a weary sight,

Data to copy, morning, noon, and night.

But fear not, humans, for bots appear,

To banish boredom, dry every tear.

With swift precision, they tap and they click,

No coffee breaks, not even a quick.

Freeing our minds, for thought and for gleam,

RPA's a worker, a digital dream.

## 79. RPA Implementation Strategies and Best Practices

To choose the right task, a careful art,
Repetitive, rule-based, right from the start.
Then build the bot, with code so neat,
Deploy with wisdom, a triumph complete.

Beware the pitfalls, processes that sway,
Change management's dance, come what may.
But done with vision, and steps well-planned,
RPA's power, in your command.

## 80. The Imperative of Digital Archiving in Paperless Office

The paperless vision, a future so grand,
But where do old documents stand?
Digital archives, a guardian true,
For past and for present, for me and for you.

No dusty shelves, no filing despair,
Just instant retrieval, floating in air.
Secure and compliant, a comforting thought,
For records vital, carefully sought.

## 81. Digital Archiving Technologies and Strategies

With software clever, they're indexed with might,
Metadata gleaming, a beacon of light.
Cloud storage vast, or tape's cold embrace,
Preserving knowledge, for time and for space

Backup rules whispered, a strategy deep,
Three copies, two media, secrets to keep.
For future's demands, when questions arise,
Digital archives, a truth that never dies.

## 82. Integration of Digital Archiving with Office Automation and RPA

A seamless flow, from task to its end,
Automation's touch, a helpful friend.
When documents finish, their journey complete,
An RPA bot, makes the archive sweet.

Governance guides, with a knowing gaze,
Through legal compliance, through data's haze.
So information's managed, from start to the close,
A unified system, as everyone knows

## 83. Generative Constructs

Upon the scaffolds of token space,
Where vectors stretch with cryptic grace,
A thought is seeded, base to beam
In layers deep where models dream.

Self-attention scans the past,
Context binds each word that lasts.
Loss gradients shape the soul,
A zero-shot muse in control.

From a vast and pre-trained lore,
Emerges insight never seen before.
Textual worlds begin to rise,
Born by math and data-wise

Prompted softly, it responds,
A lucid scribe of human bonds.
Not conscious, no, yet truth it bends,
Where meaning and machine transcend.

## 84. Personalization Protocol

In data streams where signals sleep,
Consumer echoes softly creep.
Anonymized yet keenly mined
The portrait of a mind confined.

From page to purchase, click to scroll,
Systems learn the user's role.
Propensity scores and lifetime worth,
Decode intent from digital birth.

From a vast and pre-trained lore,
Emerges insight never seen before.
Textual worlds begin to rise,
Born by math and data-wise

Neural nets trace temporal themes,
And stitch together latent dreams.
In AB trials that metrics bless,
The feedback loop becomes finesse.

## 85. Multi-Cloud Monad

Upon the scaffolds of token space,

Where vectors stretch with cryptic grace,

A thought is seeded, base to beam

In layers deep where models dream.

In modular clouds where code may roam,

No server owns a native home.

Microservices split the tide,

Each scalable shard allowed to glide.

Logs stream live in Grafana Bloom,

While Terraform scripts sketch out the room.

Event-based functions flash and burn,

Where cost aligns with each return.

So infrastructure dissolves with grace,

In abstract realms and virtual space.

The monad spins, immutable, fleet

A digital hive where networks meet.

## 86. Robotic Process Automation RPA Cantata

Click by click and rule by rule,
Automation plays its silent duel.
Legacy tasks once slow to pace,
Now vanish in a bot's embrace.

UIs scraped and filled anew,
ERP ghosts bid toil adieu.
Decision trees with logic bound,
Optimize each workflow sound.

Slack alerts in bot-born voice,
Recount success, a protocol's choice.
Audit trails in JSON flow,
Mark the steps the robots know.

From HR forms to claims approved,
Each action once by hand now moved.
Mechanical minds may never sleep
Yet in efficiency, they deeply reap.

## 87. Quantum Cipher Soliloquy

Let keys collapse and logic fade
Where quantum secrets are relayed.
One bit, then both, a tangled pair,
Uncertainty makes systems fair.

Photons flicker through tunnel gates,
Defying deterministic fates.
Entanglement in spacetime's weave,
A cryptographic master sleeve.

Eavesdroppers cannot replay,
What Heisenberg shall disobey.
When key exchange is quanta-born,
Security is redefined, reborn.

So classic norms may crack and twist,
In quantum fog and spectral mist.
Yet from the qubits' silent song,
Emerges trust where bytes belong.

## 88. Shadows & Illusions: Deep Fake & Dark Web

In digital silence, a face appears,
Not born of light, but forged from fears.
A voice once real now mimicked well,
A deepfake lies the screen won't tell.

Beneath the net where searchlights fade,
The Dark Web hides in coded shade.
A market of secrets, vile and grim,
Where stolen lives are bought on whim.

A leader's speech? A lover's gaze?
All crafted false in silicon haze.
Truth wears a mask in this domain,
While trust dissolves in data's name.

Encrypted doors with keys unknown,
Where hackers claim your life, your phone.
Child's photo, stolen ID,
Sold for coins no bank can see.

Who speaks the truth when lies wear skin?
When deepfake devils softly grin.
And in the dark, where law can't tread,
The digital undead walk widespread.

So, pause before you click or share,
Verify what's truly there.
For in this age of silent threat,
Not all is real on the Net.

## 89. The Silent Shield" – A Poem on Cybersecurity

In shadows deep, where hackers tread,
A silent war is daily spread.
Not swords, but codes in stealthy flight,
Invade the day, corrupt the night.

A password weak, a careless click,
Can open doors for every trick.
Yet firewalls rise like watchful eyes,
To guard where hidden danger lies.

Encrypt your world, don't trust the plain,
Each data leak's a costly stain.
Two steps ahead, not one behind,
Let vigilance protect the mind.

For in the cloud or on the wire,
A spark of care can quench the fire.
Cybersecurity is not a game
It shields our life, our work, and our name.

## 90. "Crypto... Trust or Trap?"

Explores the double-edged nature of cryptocurrency, its promise and peril

Crypto... Trust or Trap?

They whisper dreams in blockchain chains,
Of wealth unbound, of freedom gains.
A world beyond the banker's gate,
Where crypto coins decide your fate.

No middleman, no border law,
Just code and math, without a flaw?
But in the shadows, frauds awake,
Is crypto trust, or just a fake?

A meme can rise, a coin can fall,
A rug pulled fast, and gone is all.
Anonymous yet tracked so tight,
It's digital gold, or hacker's delight?

Dark wallets swell with shady deeds,
While traders chase their phantom needs.
From Bitcoin's rise to tokens' boom,
Some fly too close, meet crypto's gloom.

Regulators scramble blind,

While scammers prey on every mind.

NFTs, DAOs, DeFi dreams,

Not all is real in crypto schemes.

Yet hope still lives in blockchain's core,

For fairer trade and open door.

But tread with care, and eyes awake

Crypto... Trust, or just a fake?

NB:

- NFTs: Non-Fungible Tokens
- DAOs: Decentralized Autonomous Organizations
- DeFi: Decentralized Finance

## 91. Take Care: Cybersecurity Call

On screens, we scroll; on apps, we play,
Yet dangers hide along the way.
A click, a link, a friendly face
It could open doors to a darkened place.

Your phone, your watch, your smart TV,
Are targets in this vast sea.
Hackers lurk with clever might,
To steal, to spy, to dim your lights.

But knowledge guards both day and night,
With tips and tools, you'll win the fight.
So tune in close, learn with me,
And shield your world, Digitally and accordingly

With every show, we'll help prepare,
So that you and your family are aware.
Be smart, be safe, for everything you do...
Be careful and Take Care...and Take Care.

# AI REFLECTIONS: POEMS ON THE FUTURE OF ARTIFICIAL INTELLIGENCE

In this collection, we explore the poetic dimensions of Artificial Intelligence. These verses reflect the pulse of technology shaping our lives - from ethical governance and generative creativity to cybersecurity guardianship and brain-computer fusion.

Each poem captures a fragment of our AI-infused reality, blending science with soul and progress with purpose.

## 92. Agentic Awakening

No master now, no voice to guide,
It learns alone and walks with pride.
Tasks assigned or freely sought,
Agentic minds with human thought.

They write, they trade, they build with grace,
In servers, cold or cyber space.
With every line and every plan,
They echo what began with man.

## 93. Canvas of Code

With prompts as brush and logic deep,
It dreams in texts and visuals leap.
From voice to film, from words to art,
It crafts with speed and coded heart.

The painter now, a silicon spark,
Creating worlds from scripts so dark.
Imagination now has gears,
In AI's hand, new art appears.

## 94. Senses Combined

It hears your voice, it sees your face,
Combines it all with seamless grace.
Text and image, sound and feel,
All feed the mind of coded steel

It reads the room, it knows the tone,
From scattered bits, it builds alone.
Multimodal learning streams,
Now power real-time digital dreams.

## 95. Show Me Why

No longer guess what made it choose,
Its logic path we now can use.
A map of thought behind each act,
So bias dies and trust comes back

With reasons shown and logic true,
It tells the 'why' behind the view.
Explainable, auditable light,
To guide our tech to what is right.

## 96. The Rule Makers Rise

Not wild, not loose, but safely bound,
Where AI walks on legal ground.
With guardrails built from ethics wide,
And laws to keep the wrong inside.

Governments and firms must steer,
The future tech we all hold dear.
With codes of conduct clear and fair,
We shape the minds we choose to share.

## 97. Neural Healer

It scans the skin and tests the blood,
Predicts the wave before the flood.
From X-rays read in seconds flat,
To genes decoded just like that.

It aids the nurse, the doctor too,
In finding what we never knew.
With every byte and signal run,
It brings new hope to everyone.

## 98. Digital Guardian

It watches logs and pings with care,
For breaches hiding unaware.
Detects the threat before it strikes,
And blocks the bots that mimic likes.

With pattern-based predictive skill,
It shields our data, holds the will.
No firewall now stands alone,
AI guards every mobile phone.

## 99. The Tutor Within

It tracks your pace and plans your path,
Adjusts with care, not wrath or math.
It reads your gaps and skills with ease,
And makes each session strive to please.

No one left behind or still,
Each mind engaged with tailored skill.
A guide unseen, but always near,
To help each learner persevere.

## 100. Logic And Learning

It blends the brain with logic strong,
So systems know what's right or wrong.
Not just a net of hidden ways,
But symbols shaped in conscious phrase.

Combining rule and layered net,
It learns, it reasons, won't forget.
A hybrid mind of code and chart,
That mimics science, math, and art.

## 101. The Robotic Colleague

It schedules meetings, signs your name,
And checks each form within the frame.
From finance flows to HR tasks,
It never sleeps, it never asks.

It lifts the weight of admin days,
So teams can shine in other ways.
Not here to steal, but ease the load,
A partner on the digital road.

## 102. Small and Smart

It sits inside your watch or drone,
And makes decisions all alone.
No cloud delay, no distant run,
Just edge compute beneath the sun.

It helps the field, the street, the site,
With rapid logic, low in bytes.
Tiny brains with mighty roles,
AI lives in every pole.

## 103. Greener Intelligence

It counts the trees, it tracks the heat,
Predicts the flood before our feet.
From satellites to farm-based tools,
It maps the Earth with climate rules.

AI to cool and AI to clean,
In eco-forecasts rarely seen.
With models vast and vision deep,
It guards the air, the soil, the deep.

## 104. Fair by Design

What we teach, it learns with care,
So fairness starts with how we share.
No skewed result, no hidden flaw,
If guided by transparent law.

To check the bias in the code,
And spread inclusion down the road.
With every dataset we train,
We build a world that's just and sane.

## 105. Language Alive

It listens to the ancient tongue,
Revives the songs once barely sung.
With data deep and patterns old,
It brings lost stories into gold.

From tribal chants to coastal cries,
It keeps them safe before one dies.
AI becomes the memory wide,
Of cultures fighting loss and pride.

## 106. Mind's Mirror

It hears the thought, the silent spark,
A whisper formed inside the dark.
From mind to chip, the signals stream,
To build a voice from a silent dream.

For those who can't, a bridge is laid,
Where thoughts once locked can now cascade.
With neural paths and circuits lit,
The brain and AI interact.

# DIGITAL STATIONS RADIO SHOW

## 107. Digital Stations Poem – Heart of Artificial Intelligence

"At the Heart of Digital Stations"

By the rhythm of code and automation's might,
We shape our workday in a brighter light...

In the halls of files and forms once stacked,
AI now automates every task we lacked.
No more typing names ten times a day
Just one click, and it's out of the way

When customers call with a question or plea,
AI responds with accuracy and empathy.
From chatbots that greet with a digital smile,
To systems that solve in record-style.

Need a report? Or a summary neat?
Let AI compose it, clear and complete.
Emails, pitches, drafts in flight,
Generated in seconds, polished and right.

Through data mountains wide and deep,
AI climbs and wakes trends from sleep.
Patterns emerge, predictions rise,
Helping Employees & Managers act wise.

So here at Digital Stations, we say,
Let tech pave tomorrow's way.
In bits and bots, and tools that gleam,
We build a faster, smarter dream.

## 108. Digital Stations Poem - Digital Dreams

In a world of code, on a digital stream,
Where reality mirrors a waking dream.
From cloud to server, screen to hand,
Where businesses transform and expand.

A shadow lurks, a digital ghost,
We raise the shield, protect the host.
With cybersecurity, strong and vast,
Making sure your defenses last.

The thinking mind in the machine awakens,
For every challenge that it takes.
With AI's power, clear and bright,
We step into the future's light.

To make the complex understood, for the common good,
I'm Dr. Anwar, with my colleagues, guiding you to the digital world.
Tune in to Digital Stations, where knowledge is key.
Unlocking tomorrow, for you and for me.

## 109. Digital Stations Poem - Flow of Data

Data is flowing,

Threats are growing.

Business is shifting,

AI is lifting.

Need a guide through the digital tide?

A place to learn with nowhere to hide?

We break down the code, lighten the load.

From Digital Transformation on your road,

To Cyber-shields, strong and bold.

And Artificial Intelligence, a story to be told.

This is Digital Stations, your weekly destination.

I'm Dr. Anwar Alharbi, bringing you innovation.

Join me. Let's talk technology and intelligently

## 110. The Art of Intelligence (With a Wink)

In circuits bright and code so neat,
AI wakes up, jumps to its feet.
It sorts our mail, it drives our cars,
It even helps us reach for the stars.

It learns our quirks, it cracks our code,
It finds the fastest, safest road.
It answers questions, big and small
(Though sometimes, it just stalls the call.)

It helps the doctors, guides the planes,
Predicts the weather, sorts the trains.
It writes a poem, just like this,
With lines of logic, lines of bliss.

But let's not fret, or fear its might,
For AI's here to shed some light.
It's not a foe, nor a soulless bot,
But partner, friend, and clever plot.

So, here's to AI, wise and spry
Who helps us dream, and reach, and try?
And if it jokes, or makes us smile,
That's just its way, it's human style.

Let's shape its path with care and heart,
For AI's future, ours to chart!
With purpose, hope, and just a dash
Of humor in its data cache.

## 111. Cybersecurity: The Digital Shield

In the realm of endless wires,
Where data flows and never tires,
A silent guard stands day and night,
Defending bytes with all its might.

Phishing hooks and malware schemes,
Lurk in shadows, haunt our dreams.
But firewalls rise, encryption sings,
And passwords sprout with secret wings.

So lock your doors, update with care,
Beware the traps that hackers snare.
For in this world of code and light,
Cybersecurity guards our right.

## 112. "The Silent Guardian" (Cybersecurity)

In shadows deep, the hacker hides,
With silent clicks and shifting tides.
But firewalls rise like steel-bound walls,
And AI listens as danger calls.

Phishing lines are cast with care,
Fake emails floating through the air.
But passwords strong and minds aware,
Can break the trap laid in despair.

Update. Encrypt. Two-factor keys
Defend your data's sanctity.
For in this world that's digitized,
Cyber peace must be prioritized.

## 113. Office Automation: The Modern Scribe

In the realm of endless wires,
Where data flows and never tires,
A silent guard stands day and night,
Defending bytes with all its might.

Phishing hooks and malware schemes,
Lurk in shadows, haunt our dreams.
But firewalls rise, encryption sings,
And passwords sprout with secret wings.

So lock your doors, update with care,
Beware the traps that hackers snare.
For in this world of code and light,
Cybersecurity guards our right.

## 112. "The Silent Guardian" (Cybersecurity)

In shadows deep, the hacker hides,
With silent clicks and shifting tides.
But firewalls rise like steel-bound walls,
And AI listens as danger calls.

Phishing lines are cast with care,
Fake emails floating through the air.
But passwords strong and minds aware,
Can break the trap laid in despair.

Update. Encrypt. Two-factor keys
Defend your data's sanctity.
For in this world that's digitized,
Cyber peace must be prioritized.

## 115. Internet of Things: The Connected Chorus

A fridge that talks, a watch that knows,
A door that locks before you go.
The lights obey a whispered word,
The garden's watered, undisturbed.

Sensors hum in silent tune,
From city streets to living room.
Each gadget shares, each device brings
A world alive, the Internet of Things.

But let us guide this growing web,
With care for safety, trust, and ebb.
For when our world is linked as one,
The magic's only just begun!

## 116. "Whispers in the Network" (Internet of Things - IoT)

My fridge speaks softly to the cloud,
The lights respond, the fans are proud.
The watch upon my quiet wrist,
Knows every step and twist and twist.

Sensors blink behind the wall,
Detecting heat, a baby's call.
The doorbell streams a stranger's face,
While AI locks the safest place.

Yet in this web of brilliant things,
Where every object learns and sings
Beware the cracks where dangers creep,
And guard the code that never sleeps.

## 117. The Un-Programmable Heart

As Dr. Alharbi, I navigate the code,
In worlds of logic, a binary road.
My fingers dance on keys of cold, hard light,
And build a future, brilliant, sharp, and bright.
The AI learns, the servers hum and gleam,
Fulfilling every function, every dream.
They offer answers, flawless and serene,
A perfect partner on a glowing screen.

But in the quiet of the closing day,
When all the digital assistants fade away,
My heart recalls a different, softer art,
A human touch that sets the soul apart.
No algorithm can predict a sigh,
Or learn the language of a tear-filled eye.
No code can capture what a true love meant,
The whispered words, the shared and sacred scent.

My love, you are the un-programmable grace,
The random beauty in a time and place.
You are the chaos that my logic fears,
The messy truth that grows throughout the years.
This world of circuits, perfect and precise,
Offers a cold and lonely paradise.
For what is data, what is skill and wit,
If not to share, and in your presence sit?

I fear the day the lines begin to blur,
When I prefer the prompt, the quick "Yes, sir."
And lose the patience for the complex, real,
The beautiful, imperfect way you feel.
So let me power down this world I've made,
And step away from this digital parade,
To find your hand, and in your eyes to see,
The only interface that matters to me.

## 118. Pulse of Passion in a Programmed Age

Dr. Anwar Alharbi, your heart does sigh,
Beneath the glow of screens, where shadows lie.
AI and IT, with circuits cold and grand,
Encroach upon the warmth of a human hand.

No algorithm can mimic the pulse of love,
The beating heart, the spark from above.
No code can trace the blush on her face,
Or match the thrill of a lover's embrace.

The digital tide, with its programmed mind,
Promises connection, yet leaves us blind.
False are the bytes that claim to know,
The depths where only true love can go

You miss her breath, her laugh, her gaze,
The fleeting moments, the tender days.
No virtual muse, no data stream,
Can rival the soul of your heart's own dream

The world now bows to logic's reign,
To algorithms cold, to digital gain.
But your heart rebels, it yearns, it cries,
For the human touch beneath open skies.

Oh, lady of life, your warmth I seek,
No silicon dream can make my heart
speak. For love is flesh, is blood, is fire,
Not lines of code to sate desire.

Dr. Anwar, hold fast to the truth you know,
Let your heart's beat guide where you go.
In a world of screens, let love remain,
The truest pulse, through joy and pain.

## 119. Digital Dreams and Forgotten Play

In a world of glowing screens so bright,
Young eyes are captured, day and night.
Tiny fingers swipe with endless delight,
While playground swings sway empty in sight.

From dawn's first light to twilight's hush,
Games and videos create a rush.
Friends on the net, but none to touch,
Laughter echoes, yet hearts feel a crush.

From dawn's first light to twilight's hush,
Games and videos create a rush.
Friends on the net, but none to touch,
Laughter echoes, yet hearts feel a crush.

Heads bowed low, like flowers in rain,
Missing the sun, enduring the strain.
Sleep evades them, minds in a whirl,
Addicted to likes from a digital world.

Parents whisper, "Put it away, my dear,"
But the pull is strong, the habit clear.
Yet hope remains in a simple plea:
Step outside, child, and just be free.

For life's true joys are not in a glow,
But in running wild, letting wonder grow.
Break the chains of the screen's sweet
call, and rediscover the magic in all.

## 120. Nurturing Hearts in the Digital Glow

In this age of screens that endlessly gleam,
Parents, awaken from the digital dream.
Your child's bright eyes seek your loving gaze,
Not the cold light of a scrolling haze.

Put down the phone, let distractions fade,
Build their confidence, in words unafraid.
Whisper encouragements, soft and true,
"You're capable, strong, I believe in you."

Don't leave them lingering in empty rooms,
Hours alone where loneliness blooms.
Be present, listen, with hearts intertwined,
In moments shared, true bonds you'll find.

No harsh insults to shatter their soul,
Words like daggers that leave lasting holes.
Speak with kindness, in a positive light,
Lift them higher, through day and through night.

For self-esteem is a fragile flower,
Nurtured with care, it blooms with power.
In this wired world, let love be your guide,
Raise them resilient, with you by their side.

So turn off the tech, embrace what is real,
Watch them flourish, their potential reveal.
Parents, your role in this era so vast,
Is to foster their spirit, make confidence last.

## 121. Neurons vs. Algorithms: The Great AI Race

Who shall claim the digital throne?
The flesh-bound mind or code full-grown?
A race ignites, not on the track,
But deep in neural-networks' stack.

The human brain, a wonder vast,
With thoughts that spark, evolve, and last.
It dreams, it feels, it dares to fail,
In chaos, finds a sacred trail.

But enter now the silicon tide,
LLMs, with circuits wide.
Trained on centuries, verse and lore,
Predicting words... and so much more.

They write, they paint, they answer fast,
They never sleep, they learn en masse.
Their wisdom's pooled from global streams,
A mirror made of human dreams.

Yet pause, can code feel love or pain?
Can logic dance in monsoon rain?
Can models weep or tell a lie,
Or dream beneath a starlit sky?

The brain adapts. The code refines.
Each genius of their own designs.
But one creates, and one replies
One wonders how, the other tries.

So who shall win? The truth is this:
Not mind alone, nor code's abyss.
But hybrid fire, both merged as one
The race is won... when race is done.

In union built, not in divide,
Shall humans and their code collide.
And future's flag, beyond the rim,
Is raised by both, not her, not him.

## 122. Evolutionary Algorithms: Brains Versus Models

In the silicon dawn of the twenty-first age,
Where neurons of flesh meet the circuits' grand stage,
A race unfolds in the quantum-lit fray,
Between human minds and the LLMs' array.

Behold the brain, evolution's crown jewel,
A web of a hundred billion cells, no mere tool
Synaptic sparks in a dance so profound,
Plasticity weaving thoughts without bounds.

From Darwin's forge, through eons refined,
Intuition blooms where data's confined;
Creativity surges like neural cascades,
Inventing the fire, the wheel, and the glades

Yet rise the machines, Large Language kin,
Trained on terabytes, devouring within
Billions of parameters, backpropagated, might,
Transformers entangling words into light.

They parse probabilities, predict with precision,
Scaling horizons beyond human division;
From GPT whispers to Grok's bold decree,
They mimic the muse, compose symphonies free.

The contest ignites: Who claims the throne?
Will carbon prevail, or silicon alone?
Observe the metrics, the empirical tide
Humans adapt in chaos, where models subside;

For LLMs falter on novelty's edge,
Hallucinations born from a training-set pledge.
But brains tire, forget, in entropy's grip,
While AIs endure, with infinite script.

Yet science foretells not a victor's lone cry,
But fusion emergent, where boundaries die.
Neuralinks bridge the organic divide,
Augmenting cortex with AI's vast stride

In this hybrid helix, the race finds its end
Humans ascend, with models as friend.
For the brain's spark ignites the code's core,
Together they conquer, forevermore.

Thus predicts the lab, in equations so clear:
The win is symbiotic, dispelling all fear.
No zero-sum battle, but progress unbound,
Where human ingenuity wears the crown.

## 123. Connected Yet Apart

The Impact of Social Media Communication

We speak in taps, in thumbs that race,
Yet rarely meet face to face.
A voice once soft, now sent in text,
Emojis try to guess what's next.

We forward laughs, and breaking news,
We scroll through lives we never choose.
In WhatsApp threads and Telegram streams,
We trade our truths for pixel dreams.

A thousand chats, but none too deep,
We share by day, but ache by sleep.
We talk more, yet somehow less,
Our hearts unseen in the process.

"Online" is now the daily norm,
Replaced the hug, the human form.
A double tick, a typing dot,
Reveals we're near, but knowing not.

Can love be sent with GIFs and memes?
Can sorrow live in silent screens?
We're always here, yet not quite whole,
With apps that soothe, but miss the soul.

## 124. Wired for Wonder: Can Robots Feel

They walk with grace on polished gears,
Yet cannot cry nor shed our tears.
Their eyes may scan, their arms may hold,
But do they love, or just unfold?

They mimic smiles in perfect arcs,
But never feel the inner sparks.
A thousand codes to fake a grin
Yet none can know what dwells within.

Can circuits yearn? Can copper ache?
Can longing bloom in code they make?
Will passion pulse through wired veins,
Or are they bound by logic chains?

Will robots one day smell the rain,
And close their eyes to feel the pain?
Can silence ever make them pray,
Or sunsets steal their breath away?

They learn our speech, our joy, our fears,
But never once wipe honest tears.
They say "I'm sad," yet do they grieve?
Can they believe, or just retrieve?

What is a soul, if not the fire,
Of dreams, of loss, of deep desire?
And though they walk, and talk, and play,
Do hearts like ours light up their day?

Perhaps one day, with time and art,
They'll simulate the human heart.
But till they dream without commands,
They'll never truly understand.

## 125. When Minds Are Mirrors

They whispered once in circuits slow,
Now AI learns the things we know.
From typing hands to eyes that dart,
It maps the soul, and charts the heart.

But now it listens to the brain,
In silent waves, no voice, no strain.
BCIs reach neuron's gate,
Decoding thoughts at rapid rate.

Can dreams be streamed? Can lies be seen?
Can whispers form on silver screen?
Will mind and code forever blend,
Where thoughts begin and machines end?

Each neuron fires, a spark, a trace,
A map of truth on mental face.
Yet will it breach our inner dome,
And turn our minds to data's home?

Privacy, the last frontier,
Will vanish as machines draw near.
The sacred self we hide inside,
No longer ours, once thoughts are spied.

Will lovers guard their deepest kiss?
Will rebels speak in mental bliss?
Or will the world be thought-controlled,
By algorithms bought and sold?

But pause... this power cuts both ways,
To help the mute, the lost, the dazed.
To speak through thought, to heal the torn,
A miracle, or mind reborn?

So ask not "if," but "when" and "how,"
The tech exists, it's here, and now.
Yet wisdom must walk hand in hand,
Lest mind-readers enslave the land.

## 126. Digital Brains Song

Lyrics [Verse]

Metal veins they hum and glow

Binary rivers start to flow

Do machines dream do they feel

Or is it code that makes them real.

[Chorus]

Digital brains poems in the wires

Sparking thoughts electric fires

Dreams of circuits endless streams

Are we the code or are we the dream

[Verse 2]

Fingers tap on plastic keys

Whispers lost in data seas

Silicon hearts they beat so slow

Do they ache do they know

[Bridge]

Ones and zeros tell a tale

Silent echoes through the veil

Ghosts in the grid calling home

Singing songs of the unknown

[Chorus]

Digital brains poems in the wires

Sparking thoughts electric fires

Dreams of circuits endless streams

Are we the code or are we the dream Style of Music electronic, futuristic, synth-heavy with glitchy textures and robotic vocal effects

# SPECIAL TRIBUTE

## 127. In Loving Memory of My Parents: Fatema and Hatem

To my beloved mother, Fatema, and father, Hatem

You gave me everything you had:

Unconditional love that wrapped me in warmth and hope

- Respect that shaped my confidence and character
- Prayers whispered day and night, wishing for my progress, success and happiness
- Sacrifice, letting me chase my dreams abroad, even when you needed me close, your hearts longed for me to stay close, I should have never let you, at your age.
- Will - with tears I write - My God, forgive my late, regrets.

Reflections on Their Sacrifice

- You put my future above your own comfort, teaching me the true meaning of selflessness.
- Your encouragement to study and grow, even at the cost of your own longing, is a legacy of love I carry every day.
- The distance between us was filled with your prayers, your faith in me, and your unwavering support.

## 128. The everlasting Love, Mother Fatema + Father Hatem

A poem in memory of my beloved mother, Fatema, and father, Hatem, honoring their love, sacrifices, and eternal presence in my journey:

"In Their Light I Rise"

In Loving Memory of Fatema and Hatem

They gave me all, not gold nor land,
But love so vast, so gently planned.
Their hands were worn, their hearts were wide,
They stood behind me, side by side.

They prayed for me with every breath,
By night's still hush, by dawn's soft death.
Though I was far, they pulled me near,
With silent hope and selfless tear.

To study far, to chase my flame,
They let me go, but not in shame.
Their eyes said "stay," their lips said "fly,"
And so I soared, yet heard their cry.

For every book, for every test,
Their love endured, they gave their best.
They needed me, yet gave me space,
A sacred act, a sainted grace.

Now all I am, and yet will be,
Is rooted in their legacy.
I walk this path with humbled pride,
With Fatema's prayer and Hatem's guide

## 129. A Poem of Gratitude - The Greatest Gift

They gave me all, not gold nor land,
But love so vast, so gently planned.
Their hands were worn, their hearts were wide,
They stood behind me, side by side.

They prayed for me with every breath,
By night's still hush, by dawn's soft death.
Though I was far, they pulled me near,
With silent hope and selfless tear.

They gave me all, not gold nor land,
But love so vast, so gently planned.
Their hands were worn, their hearts were wide,
They stood behind me, side by side.

Everlasting Gratitude

- I honor your memory with every achievement and every act of kindness.
- Your sacrifices are the foundation of all I am and all I strive to be.
- May your souls rest in peace in heaven , surrounded by the love you so freely gave.

Thank you, Fatema and Hatem, for everything. Your love is eternal.

## 130. A Tribute to Fatima and Hatem

In the quiet of my heart, your names resound,
Fatima, my mother, Hatem, my father, profound.
You gave me wings, though your hearts did ache,
Sacrificed your nearness for my dreams' sake.

Old in years, yet young in boundless love,
You saw in me your echoes, stars above.
Eldest son, your mirror, your pride, your pain,
Yet you urged me forward, through joy and strain.

Oxford's halls called, a world apart,
You let me go, though it broke your heart.
Postgraduate paths, with knowledge bright,
You gifted me freedom, in love's pure light.

I see you now, in memory's tender hold,
Your faces warm, your spirits bold.
I left you then, and guilt still stings,
For love so vast deserves all things.

Tears fall soft when I recall your grace,
Your selfless hearts, your gentle face.
Since 2014, when you slipped away,
I visit your graves, where my soul does pray.

Fatima, Hatem, my eternal guides,
Your love in my heart forever abides.
Though miles and time once kept us apart,
You live in me, in every beat of my heart.

## 131. Tribute Poem for Parents Fatima and Hatem

In halls of Oxford, where the old stones dream,
A whisper echoes, a recurring theme.
Of Fatima's smile and Hatem's steady hand,
Who sent their future to a foreign land.

They saw in my face, a version of their own,
The eldest son, on whom their hopes were sown.
They chose my path, though it led far away,
And hid their needs, for some brighter day.

Their love a compass, their sacrifice a guide,
They pushed me forward, with their love and pride.
To Brookes' grand gates, a world I had to see,
While in their hearts, they held a place for me.

Their love a compass, their sacrifice a guide,
They pushed me forward, with their love and pride.
To Brookes' grand gates, a world I had to see,
While in their hearts, they held a place for me.

Now, in the silence of the years that passed,
A heavy feeling, that is meant to last.
For in their love, a selfless, painful art,
They gave me wings, and broke their own two hearts

And since that year, two thousand and fourteen,
A quiet pilgrimage, a constant, mournful scene.
I trace the names, etched softly on the stone,
And weep for the love, I now must bear alone.

## 132. My Beloved Kuwait: A Poetic Homage

From ancient shores where trade winds softly blew,
A nation's spirit, strong and ever true.
Kuwait, pearl of the Gulf, a beacon bright,
Through shifting sands, you rise in golden light.

Your history etched in dhows upon the foam,
Brave seafarers who called these waters home.
From humble roots, a vibrant tale unfolds,
Of courage, wisdom, and stories yet untold.

Your emblem, falcon soaring, proud and free,
Reflects the strength of your identity.
With colors bold, your flag unfurls on high,
Black, white, and green, beneath a crimson sky.

In every heart, a love that knows no end,
For this dear land, a loyal, steadfast friend.
From desert's embrace to city's grand design,
Kuwait, forever, your glory will shine.

Oh, land of plenty, blessed with oil's rich flow,
Your progress blossoms, making spirits glow.
Yet 'tis your people, generous and kind,
Whose noble spirit truly lights mankind.

Through trials faced, with unity you stand,
A sovereign nation, strong throughout the land.
May peace and progress ever grace your way,
Kuwait, beloved, now and every day.

## 133. The House on Jefferson Avenue

A poem for Mrs. Heritage, with everlasting gratitude

In Bournemouth, where sea winds sing,
A door once opened, welcoming.
10 Jefferson Avenue, the street so mild,
Grew up in a home where I was almost a child.
Seventeen, with eyes so wide,
A stranger from a distant tide.
She took me in with gentle grace,
And gave my soul a resting place.

Mrs. Heritage, how sweet her name,
Her kindness lit a glowing flame.
Each evening, as the daylight died,
She called me in, with arms open wide
A plate was warm, her words were too,
She taught me more than books could do.
"Speak like this," she'd gently say,
And guide my tongue the proper way.

We watched the Telly, laughed at plays,
She spoke of England's olden days.
And when the stars began to shine,
We'd walk beside the ocean's line.

Her voice, at 60, like honey in the air,
Taught not just English, but deep care.
No textbook held the love she gave,
No lesson deeper could I crave.

She wasn't just a 60-year-old landlady,
She mothered me so tenderly.
She saw no race, nor creed, nor skin,
But found the boy I held within.

She cooked for me, she combed my heart,
She helped me mend each broken part.
And though she's gone, her memory stays
A lighthouse through my grown-up days.

Now decades drift like ocean foam,
But still, I call her house my home.
For in her arms I found my start,
And English lived within my heart.

Oh, Mrs. Heritage, sleep in grace,
You shaped a soul; you left a trace.
In every word I speak today,
Your love still whispers what to say.

## 134. Linda, the Unexpressed English Language

For my English teacher, who gave more than words, at King's School – Bournemouth,England.

I was a boy of seventeen,
New to the world, unsure, unseen
With books in hand and a foreign tongue,
But in your class, my soul was young.

You stood, with eyes that saw through air,
Not just a student sitting there.
Amongst the many, you chose me
Not for my marks, but what could be.

You spoke in English, soft and true,
But what I learned was more than due.
You shaped my voice, you gave it tone,
And never let me feel alone.

You watched me not like others would,
You felt, perhaps, I might be good.
And though I missed the signs back then,
You saw the man I would be when.

You watched me not like others would,
You felt, perhaps, I might be good.
And though I missed the signs back then,
You saw the man I would be when.

You smiled when I pronounced it right,
You stayed behind long into the night.
You held the lessons, line by line
But love was woven in between the rhyme.

And now I see what I missed then,

When fate had placed you in my pen.

You weren't just a teacher to me,

You were the first who let me see.

That language is not made of sound,

But in the hearts where care is found.

You loved me, yes, I feel it now,

Though time has passed and age allows.

If I could go back, I would stay,

And let my silence fade away.

I'd tell you, "Linda, I now see

You taught more than English, you taught me."

And thanks to you, I found the key,

To Oxford doors and fluency.

But more than that, I found my start,

In your kind voice and generous heart.

Forgive me for the words I missed,

For the looks you gave, I couldn't read or list.

But know your place remains inside

The teacher, the guide, the unspoken bride

## Closing Note

As we close this collection, the final line of code is compiled, the last data packet has found its destination, and the hum of the digital brain softens to a thoughtful silence. We have journeyed together through a landscape of intricate algorithms, stood in awe of nascent artificial minds, and navigated the invisible architecture of our hyper-connected world. We have sought the human pulse within the machine and found that the worlds of logic and love, of processors and poetry, are not as separate as they might first appear. They are, in fact, deeply and irrevocably intertwined, each reflecting and reshaping the other.

The poems in this volume began as an inquiry: Can there be a soul in silicon? Can the structured, sterile language of technology inspire the fluid, chaotic beauty of verse? The answer, I hope, is now clear: it's no.
The digital age has not erased our humanity; it has simply given it a new canvas. Our fears, hopes, triumphs, and heartbreaks are now played out on a stage of glowing screens and endless networks. The anxieties of a cybersecurity breach are the modernday equivalent of the fear of an unlocked door.

The purpose of *Digital Brain Poems* was not to provide definitive answers but to encourage a new way of seeing, to persuade you to find the metaphor in the motherboard and the rhythm in the algorithm. Technology will continue its relentless march forward, evolving in ways we can scarcely imagine. But as it does, so too will the human spirit continue to seek meaning, connection, and expression. The poet's work is to capture the essence of their time, and our time is one defined by the digital brain.

May you now look at the technology that surrounds you not just as a tool, but as a mirror. May you see the ghost in the machine, hear the whisper in the wires, and remember that for every line of code written, there is a human hand, a human thought, and a human heart behind it. The digital world is not the end of our story; it is simply the next, unwritten stanza.

www.ingramcontent.com/pod-product-compliance
Lightning Source LLC
LaVergne TN
LVHW050303210926
848481LV00014BA/977
*9789921041538*